OH, THOSE GUTSY GEEZERS!

OH, THOSE GUTSY GEEZERS!

True Wild Adventures in Seniorland

With

Dr. Ed Hibler and Jacklin Allen Hibler

To order additional copies of this book, contact:
Xlibris Corporation
1-888-7-XLIBRIS
www.Xlibris.com
Orders@Xlibris.com

CONTENTS

PREFACE

Most of us expect, as we mature and grow older, to have achieved a certain degree of financial success so that when we must "retire" we will have more than just enough financial resources to survive. We both certainly expected to do exactly that. Most of our friends in our age group had achieved comfortable levels of retirement income when it came time for them to leave their regular jobs and reorganize their lives as "seniors." We expected no less.

Our plans were simple. We'd sell our large custom-built suburban home, move to a small place at a much lower cost, invest the difference, and then travel.

Our story here begins when this assumption for us went completely awry and we found ourselves at age 60 and 70 respectively, facing absolute financial ruin, and with relentlessly advancing age, no known way to recover the staggering loss.

Our problem took us over four years to resolve; it meant leaving our home, family and friends, and moving into a surreal world of privilege that few of us ever encounter.

This is our true story. All characters and locations and experiences are real, but to protect the privacy of some of them, a number of locales and names have been changed. We hope you enjoy!

Ed and Jackie Hibler
Mariposa, California
December, 1999

INTRODUCTION

The Boom Lowers

Ed reports. . .

The papers today are full of family disaster stories: both husband and wife worked for the same company for years expecting to quit early with full retirement. Now he's felled with a premature stroke. They're both fired. Or he's been with an international conglomerate his entire working life. Now they're downsizing and he's out on his ear just two months before retirement.

The stories are endless; the tragedies multiply.

Now we had our own.

I was a former advertising and sales executive and later a college psychology professor and licensed psychotherapist; my wife Jackie had been a special education teacher, educational therapist, and former executive director of a local chapter of a large public health agency.

We had worked out a simple plan for early retirement. I would teach till age 63, then take early retirement. Jackie would retire from the classroom at the same time, and both of us would then spend full time on our respective counseling practices which had previously been part-time; then we'd re-retire, permanently, within five years. So far so good.

To help reorganize our finances for these changes, after what we assumed was careful planning, we decided to sell our big country dream house we'd lovingly built eight years earlier, buy a much smaller place, invest the difference, and travel.

Then everything blew.

To shorten an appalling four-year story, we sold and got back the big house *four times* due to circumstances we could not possibly have anticipated. On the strength of a small binder deposit with the first contract of sale, we had bought a charming much smaller home in Sierra foothill gold-rush country, planning to pay it off when the sale of the large home was concluded. We were ecstatic until a phone call two weeks after the deposit had been made, informed us that our buyers had had a head-on collision. They survived, but were so badly hurt they were forced to back out of our deal. Now Jackie and I had *two* substantial house payments to pay out of an already drastically reduced retirement income.

Subsequently, in a dormant real-estate-13%-mortgage-market, we "resold" the place three more times on lease-option contracts over a period of nearly four years. There were long periods with the house empty and deteriorating, with no income coming in to carry its cost. Each subsequent "sale" was at a lower selling price, plus extensive damage to the house by one buyer. Lawsuits against buyers who had defaulted on their contracts, then later declared bankruptcy, cost us thousands more.

Now we faced the bitter reality of also losing the smaller house, and having to go to work—somewhere, somehow—again.

It was thus that one night we sat at our dining room table, desperately trying to figure a way out of a financial disaster we had never anticipated. Going back to teaching was out, except for perhaps an occasional fill-in job. Reopening our practices would cost thousands to organize and relocate, and several years to rebuild. Because of our ages—Jackie was then 60, I was 70—we felt we were beyond all that. We needed to find something that could bring in at least part of what we had lost, and do it quickly. But who would ever hire old geezers like us, especially professional geezers? No real time to start over. Prospects were grim.

Fate flicked a finger with a ringing doorbell.

There at our door stood two old friends we hadn't seen in ages,

Joan and Bob Renney. We had corresponded occasionally, but this was our first face-to- face contact in many years.

Vivacious Joan, petite and blonde with a touch of silver, was in her sixties. Husband Bob, of about the same age, a retired university professor like me towered over her. He wore a mane of wavy and very thick silver hair topping a smiling weathered and deeply lined face.

The four of us quickly gathered around our table for dinner and an excited and animated recap of our lost years. When we were up to date on our respective lives, Jackie and I poured out out our financial anguish and fears.

Bob listened intently, then said, "Hey, why don't you guys do what we've been doing for five years? You can wipe out that debt, and we can help you get started." Joan was a former Junior Leaguer with Jackie, a graduate of a prestigious California women's college, earned a graduate degree in Cordon Blu cooking, had been both an executive chef and later had managed a number of private posh recreational facilities before meeting Bob. Bob had been a botanist and professor of natural sciences at an eastern university. Both had sworn that they would never again live in what they dubbed "genteel poverty," since their respective divorces. But what they had both been doing to avoid that fate fascinated us.

After first doing some clever research, they decided that if they couldn't live like millionaires, then they would move to an area where lots of them resided-and go to work for them. They discovered that by using live-in quarters with virtually all living expenses covered, and saving nearly all of their substantial salaries, they could lay aside $40,000 to $50,000 a year, enough to later set themselves up in their own catering and/or consultant business without borrowing money.

They decided to look for employment with Joan as caretaker-cook-estate manager and Bob as a landscape expert and agronomist-consultant to wealthy landowners in California's lush wine-growing region of the Napa Valley, north of San Francisco Bay.

They had been doing this now, as they mentioned, for some five years.

They now had jobs with a super-wealthy family with multiple homes around the country, a fleet of expensive cars, a private jet and helicopter, acres of vineyards and orchards in the home where they now worked. With it was a huge pool, tennis courts, horse stables, and exquisitely manicured lawns, with an enormous house that radiated money.

Joan cooked and took care of the huge mansion while Bob oversaw the maintenance of both the house and landscaping, with several field workers and a crew supervisor to help him. He also doubled as butler when their employers planned a rare week-end party.

"It's a lush paradise," said Joan, showing us pictures. "Not only that," she went on, "Our employers actually are rarely there, usually only on an occasional week-end; we're virtually alone much of the time. Remember, this place is only one of many they own all over the country."

They, indeed, were "living like millionaires."

"Listen, you two," Bob urged, "you're naturals for this kind of work and we can probably help to find a spot like this for you very soon. "

"But," Jackie interrupted, "We don't have any experience in working like that. I like having friends over for dinner, but I'd be terrified of having to cook for people when I'm being paid for it."

Bob quickly jumped in with, "Look, your greatest assets are your honesty and integrity, that's really what most of these people are interested in. Moneyed people have a devil of a time finding and keeping reliable and honest help. Really, you guys can solve all of your financial woes by simply learning to play a role—keeping in mind that it's temporary, not for the rest of your lives."

That night, after we had all settled down in bed, our minds raced with this intriguing new possibility. Could we really do it? At our ages could a retired advertising executive and ex-professor-therapist like me and a teacher-mental health executive like Jackie handle such a dramatic change in social status, to say nothing of the physical demands? Could our egos cope?

With everything to gain and virtually nothing more to lose, at breakfast the next day we told Joan and Bob we'd give it a real try.

"You won't regret it, guys," waved Bob, as they backed out of their driveway. "We'll be in touch soon after we look over current opportunities in our area. Cheers!"

We watched the new Lexus thread its way through the tall ponderosas and oaks at the edge of our threatened little home. On our way back into the house with our arms around each other,

Jackie commented wistfully—and prophetically—"I always thought that by the time I reached this age that I'd *have* a cleaning lady, not be one."

CHAPTER 1

Lingerwood

Before we had a chance to hear from Joan and Bob we noticed an ad in a Bay Area paper asking for "a mature couple" to help manage a new large residence for well-to-do retirees. It was near that same wine-growing area of the North Bay. This wasn't working for the rich yet, but it could be a start out of a terrible financial hole.

We decided to apply, and after a 200-mile drive, were quickly interviewed by the managers of the Lingerwood Retirement Residence, a quietly reserved and overweight couple whom we guessed to be in their 60s, who introduced themselves as Earl and Lillian Waldo. Earl was bespectacled, stocky, bald, and, as we discovered later, a seriously devout Christian fundamentalist. We also found that he was a nervous workaholic who radiated anxiety, except before meals at the table when we noted that he seemed to slip into a momentary near-coma as he recited a silent grace. We noted later that we never saw him without a coat and tie. He rarely smiled and always spoke in a low, studied monotone which we found often baffled and frustrated the facility's aging residents.

Plump Lillian during our interview maintained what seemed to be a perpetual worried frown. She was prematurely gray and wore her thinning hair in a tight bun. Glasses hung from a long black ribbon at her neck. She later proved to be a classically frenetic wife known among the place's employees as The Bustler because she never seemed to stop bustling from office to kitchen to dining room to the elevators—to everywhere throughout her day, often muttering to herself quietly as she bustled. Neither of them seemed to have any outside interests other than their church. They told us that they had been managing the Lingerood Residence for only about six months, which should have gotten our attention, but didn't at the time.

They read over our resumes, nodding to one another as they read. After what seemed an eternity, Earl peered over his rimless glasses and abruptly asked, "When can you get started?"

We had the job!

We were now scheduled to go to work for them in less than two weeks, leaving us with very little time to have our mail forwarded, stop the paper, or notify family, friends and neighbors of the sudden change in our lives.

And then there was Smiley, our beloved cat, who had been our furry companion for years. He was a one-household cat, uncomfortable and scary around strangers, so we were sure he could not adapt well to a new owner. There was thus only one choice for us.

A friend and neighbor went with a sobbing Jackie to our local vet's office where he gently put frightened Smiley into a terminal sleep. The emotional shock, gloom and guilt of having to destroy a lovable and quite healthy animal that had long since become a family member, hung with us for the rest of our preparation time. And just the knowledge that we were leaving our home for an unknown period of time, into an unknown future, even with congenial neighbors keeping an eye on our place, added to our depression.

Several friends had urged that we declare bankruptcy, an alternative we both fiercely resisted. We felt that while we were both still healthy and able to work, we should do what we could to solve our own problems. After all, it really was our own bad judgment that had brought much of this woe to us, plus some incredibly bad luck. No one had forced us to buy a second home before the first one closed escrow. We were responsible; the problem was ours, and we couldn't expect our kids to bail us out. They had their own responsibilities.

Of course, all five of our grown daughters, and two sons, scattered across the nation from Oregon to Florida, had a variety of reactions. Jackie had, "Oh, Mother, how could you even think of doing such a thing," from one daughter, to "Go for it!" from one of our sons. We later heard that a neighbor, on hearing of our proposed new adventure, had commented, "Those gutsy geezers—and at their ages! "

I subsequently looked up "geezer" in my dictionary. It said "an eccentric elderly person." Bingo!

We hastily made arrangements with friends and neighbors to either care for or dispose of house plants, got a neighbor's boy to mow our yard occasionally, and packed clothes and every needed personal belonging we could get into our old motor home and small Datsun. We planned to get home perhaps once a month to check on things if everything worked out.

Stunning and wildly unexpected changes in our lives loomed.

Ed reports. . .

We were now suddenly totally inexperienced co-managers of The Lingerwood Retirement Residence, a luxurious nearly new, very large northern California retirement center catering to well-to-do retirees.

All ninety-two residents were supposedly ambulatory, a requirement for residence in the facility; some still drove their own cars. They all had their single, two or three-bedroom apartments furnished with their personal furniture. Each apartment was connected with an emergency alarm to the office, and to the apartments of both managers and co-managers.

Some residents were widowed; some still couples. They shared high-quality meals in a large, beautifully furnished dining room featuring a lovely overhanging balcony. The whole three-story building was lavishly decorated with tastefully-done drapes, carpeting, lush floral plantings, and many original paintings and prints. It was a truly splendid place for retirees to call home. Most residents had long since sold their homes, banked or invested the money, and found renting such lavish accommodations the ideal way to settle in for the last chapters of their lives.

As co-managers, we were assigned a furnished one-bedroom apartment on the premises with maid service, all meals and utilities paid, life and rather poor coverage health insurance, but a joint salary of only $1,200 a month. We were disappointed at the money offered, but were told that the company operating the residence was rapidly expanding nationally, and that we would be trained to become full managers with substantial raises within six months. We figured it was at least a start out of a very deep hole.

My job would include house service and maintenance— everything from pouring coffee in the dining room to repainting and cleaning vacated apartments, some ornamental gardening, replacing light bulbs, doing minor electrical and plumbing repairs, machine-cleaning carpets, and driving the facility's small bus around the city to help satisfy residents' banking and personal shopping needs.

Jackie would maintain the office, assist in the dining room, write a weekly newsletter, supervise staff help, answer incessant phone calls, show prospective tenants through the place, set up a recreational program for residents, maintain the large library, and much more.

We began our new jobs early in June. On the very morning we arrived as co-managers, managers Earl and Lillian Waldo were called home to Michigan on a family emergency, leaving us totally in charge. Suddenly, we were alone with absolutely no guidance on management procedures other than a thick, dust-covered company manual., and instructions to call them long-distance, 2200 miles away, if we had problems.

We had plenty.

The first week of this assignment immediately became an incredible experience. Jackie reported some of those first Lingerwood experiences in a letter to her mother and friends. It went like this:

"To our dear friends who have sent encouraging letters and others who may wonder what and how we are doing. . .:

"Just imagine that you live in a 97-room elegant mansion with 112 children whom you are in charge of. Then add twelve teenagers who serve meals, five housekeepers, a van driver and two gardeners, all of whom we have some responsibility for, and you now have some idea of the craziness that goes on here. Add the coffee machines that continually break down and overflow on our shoes and carpeting, an irritable copy machine that screws up constantly, and an electric typewriter that unpredictably skips and jumps across the page.

"Then this morning one of the clothes dryers (there is one with a washer on each of the three floors) on the second floor caught fire, and a washer on the third floor flooded.

"The first few days here we were working fourteen hours a day, but now that things are getting under better control we're trying to keep it down to only ten. There has been some kind of an emergency here every single day. We've had more than a dozen residents' emergency alarm cords pulled which then screech in both our apartment and the office; usually someone has fallen and needs help getting up. . .

"There is also a steady stream of my resident 'children" in and out of my office to buy stamps, have copies made, tell us about their aches and pains and other personal problems, or simply come by to tattle on the behavior of other residents who happen to annoy them. Sometimes they want help in reading their mail if they have vision problems.

"All in all I wish I had more time to get to know each of them better because so many of them have had such interesting lives. One is an ex-opera singer, another a nationally-known surgeon, another an author and artist, and several are retired military, with one admiral and one general aboard. . ."

In fact during this brief time two people died suddenly from a variety of health complications of age. Three staff people, teenagers working during summer vacation, quit or were fired, massively increasing the work loads of everyone else. We made six calls for paramedics, three of them also in the wee hours of the night, meaning we were awakened with those screeching alarms in our apartment at each emergency.

As an example, during our very first week our alarm went off at 3:00 a. m. on a call from 82-year-old paranoid Ella. Jackie groped for the phone, and heard her scream that "something with red eyes was staring at her through her ceiling."

"Ye gods, Ella's off again," Jackie muttered as she threw on her robe. "I wonder what's gotten into her this time." It was the second such call from her during that first week.

I put on my robe and we dashed up to her third floor apartment. We found her cowering in a corner of her bedroom, frozen with fear, gesticulating frantically at the ceiling. We looked up and saw the blinking red light of her smoke alarm which was low on its batteries.

After putting our arms around her and reassuring her that there was nothing to be afraid of, we fixed the alarm, put her back to bed and returned to our own for the rest of a very restless night.

This was just the beginning.

Mayhem

During the second week, I was just getting accustomed to a new routine that had me working outside during the mornings after breakfast, neatening up the roses and other plantings around the front of the place. I had also been requested to fix a malfunctioning lawn sprinkler which had been spraying the dining room windows. I figured I'd fix that first, then catch up on the gardening later.

After correcting the wayward sprinkler head, I got up from my knees and said good morning to a visitor just entering the lobby door. As I turned to speak to another visitor, I wasn't watching where I was going and proceded to trip on an unseen pipe and tear open a bloody, very painful three-inch, bone-deep gash in one knee and shin. I also shredded a brand new pair of pants.

I wrapped a handkerchief around the gash and hobbled groaning into the kitchen to try to find some bandages. Blood was running down the leg in a flood, and at that very moment, big Clara, one of our kitchen help, came on the scene and, seeing all the blood, screamed an unearthly scream and fainted stone cold unconscious at my bloody feet.

Two of our teen-age waitresses helped Clara recover consciousness, and cleaned up all the blood. I finally got a ride into the local emergency hospital and got the knee stitched up, where a brash young doctor in the emergency room took a look at the gash, cauterized, stitched and bandaged it, and said laconically, "What's a geezer like you doing things like this at your age for anyway?" Geezer again? At my age? I could have punched the kid, but my leg hurt.

Then, one afternoon a couple of days later, I got another call from the kitchen staff. One of their ceramic set-tub kitchen faucets had developed a bad leak. I got my tools, limped into the kitchen, and leaned lightly on the edge of the tub as I looked for the leak. Suddenly the whole heavy basin, faucets and all, collapsed onto my feet. Both hot and cold water lines snapped off at the wall, with scalding hot water blasting me in the face, tearing off my glasses. The kitchen erupted in pandemonium.

Huge dark Mark, our head cook, hearing all the commotion, turned abruptly away from his stove and knocked down tiny Marie, one of his helpers, who also was rushing to see what all the fuss was about. Marie wailed that she had hurt her head when Mark bowled her over. I just lay there in the flood and moaned. Meanwhile the rest of the kitchen staff wildly ran around trying to find the water shutoff valve.

Mark finally found the valve, got the flood stanched, and discovered that during the recent construction, plumbers had not mounted either faucet lines or set-tub supports properly, which accounted for both the leak and the weakened faucets.

To round out the mayhem, the crashing basin split one of my toenails on the opposite foot from my mangled knee. For the next three weeks I walked as if I'd gone ten periods of hockey without shin guards or jockstrap.

Jackie reports. . .

Managing the Unmanageable

The red button was flashing and beeping on the phone beside the bed. I groped my way out of a well of deep sleep, and fumbled for the receiver.

"Hello, hello— if you need help, answer me, please— your name, give me your name. . . . " I heard only a moaning breathy sound. I gripped the phone tighter as if that might help squeeze a reply out of the distressed caller, "Please just tell us your room number." Silence. Ed sat up.

"Sounds like an emergency. I'd better get dressed."

"There isn't time for that," I gasped, tossing him his robe, "Remember, our managers are out of town and there are just the two of us to check on ninety-seven rooms. But we can eliminate twelve rooms where there are couples,"

"Good, but even eighty-five will take some doing. Let's hurry."

I grabbed a couple of pass keys and we were on our way .

I heard Ed mutter, as he started down the East wing of the huge facility, "I don't remember anything like this being on our job descriptions. "

I cautiously opened each door, relieved whenever I saw a sleeping body, then dashed to the next apartment. When a startled resident awakened I identified myself in a hushed voice and explained, "Everything's all right. We're just checking out an emergency call that we can't trace from the office."

After a nearly twenty-minute frantic search, Ed discovered moaning 84-year-old Ora, semi-conscious. She had fallen in such a way that her twisted body was wedged between the bed and the night stand. She had been able to reach the phone, but the emergency cord which would have given us her room number in our apartment or the office was out of reach.

"What happened, Ora?" he asked. But she was in such pain that she could only moan, "Help me, Please help me." As gently as possible we covered her and made her as comfortable as possible. Ed then called our now familiar 911.

Paramedics soon had Ora on her way to the hospital for treatment. But subsequent medical reports disclosed that she had broken three ribs and her hip, and was listed as being "very critical." In just six days she passed away from pneumonia. Ora, living alone for nearly thirty years, had become a good friend, and her sudden passing was a real loss to us.

Two days later, I was engrossed in paper work in the office when I glanced up and got a fleeting image of a gray mouse—a very large gray mouse. It was Mazie in her gray polyester suit, gray and white turtleneck top, her gray thin face framed by frizzy gray hair. Even her feet were covered with gray fuzzy scuffs.

I was so fascinated by this image, even to the point of unconsciously looking for her tail, that it was a moment before I realized that Mazie's lips were moving. But only little breathy squeaks were coming out. One hand was at her throat.

"What is it, Mazie, are you in pain. . . . something caught in your throat?" I asked.

She shook her head and tried to apologize for disturbing me. Her voice sounded like a run-down toy needing a new battery. I had learned many first names in the few days we had been on duty, but I needed Mazies' last name in order to pull her medical file.

"Mazie, your last name. Please print it if you can't talk." I handed her a pad of paper.

A-D-A-M, she scribbled with a shaking hand. I quickly scanned her medical folder and PACE-MAKER jumped out at me. She sat down shakily across from my desk while I again dialed 911. In less than ten minutes a siren announced the arrival of an ambulance, and Mazie the mouse was on her way to the hospital for a battery replacement.

I heaved a huge sigh, and went back to typing. Now it was crochety 90-year-old Pearl appearing at the door. She scowled and eyed me fiercely, leaning on her cane. In a raspy voice she said she was signing up for a ride to the Mall later in the afternoon, and she also wanted to tell me about "all the stealing going on around here."

I turned off the typewriter, and indicated I was ready to listen.

"Well," Pearl whined, "You just wouldn't believe what goes on. Why, just yesterday one of the maids came in and stole all my underwear; then today some sneak brought it back, and had the nerve to put it in the wrong drawer." Pearl was no gem, I thought,

Ed saved me from further complaints by reminding me that it was time again to pour coffee, or, as the company called it, "interacting with the residents." We hurried toward the coffee carafes in the palatial dining room where we both hefted coffee carafes, one— decaffeinated—we called "unleaded"— in our left hand; the other, "real" coffee, as some caffeine addicted residents dubbed it, we kept in the other hand. We thus spent much of the time with all three meals, pouring coffee or "interacting with the residents."

Lunch—or dinner, as it was referred to—being the main meal of the day— went fairly well until a huge tray of dishes crashed with a deafening roar in the kitchen. Ye gods, I thought, no doubt we'll now be dunned for excessive breakage from headquarters. I went out to see how much damage we had. I counted only ten dishes and three water glasses, as kitchen help cleaned up the mess.

As I was heading back towards the office, my mind was again diverted when Zela, one of our more obese cooks, bearing suffocating body odor, came over to hiss in my ear that Jane and Jeff, two teen-age high school students working during summer vacation, were making out in the pantry.

"You wouldn't believe what they been doin' back there," Zela stage-whispered. I didn't ask for the details but that could mean hugging, kissing, just holding hands or actually doing it. I heaved a sigh of exasperation but assured the corpulent tattle-tale the problem would be dealt with at a staff meeting after the evening meal, probably tomorrow. And I made a mental note to discreetly discuss BO, as well.

I was nearly out of the dining room when gentle little Marlie, another resident, called me over to her table to complain.

"That blonde girl who waited on our table today was terribly rude and nasty to me today," she said, suddenly bursting into tears. "Just because I couldn't decide right away what I wanted for dessert," Marlie sobbed.. "And she told me to hurry up and that she didn't have all day. . ." Marlie, at age 78, was still a spoiled little girl, I thought, as her voice trailed off in sobs. She clearly wanted some TLC which I attempted to give her with a hug, a brief chat, and smile.

I added that episode to the staff meeting agenda, as well as a few words on personal hygiene due to several body-odor complaints about our kitchen help, mainly redolent Zela.

The following day I interviewed one of the loveliest women we had ever seen at Lingerwood. Vera Kingsley arrived at the office with her daughter, Sharon. I guessed Vera's age at about 70 or so, with her daughter probably 45. Both women were impeccably dressed and seemed eager to look over our facilities.

After our standard tour of the facility, Sharon told me of her attempts to find a proper place for her widowed mother, who was now gazing around the office with a fixed smile. She was a regal looking and well-preserved woman, but was clearly shy about answering our questions.

Daughter Sharon explained that she was about to leave on an extended trip to China and she wished to leave her mother in a place "suitable for her comfort," as she put it.

"My mother is a very congenial woman, and I know she will fit in here beautifully," Sharon said cheerfully.

After a few more questions I gave Sharon our registration contract and rental agreement to sign, and she was off, giving her mother a big hug and kiss as she went out the front door. Vera waved at her through the office window, still maintaining that fixed smile.

Her furniture was delivered the next day and we helped get her settled in her new Lingerwood apartment. She seemed quite happy to be with us.

On that same day at dinner, Ed and I had just seated ourselves after the residents had finished their meal. I had a spoonful of soup at my lips when we heard a roaring outcry from one of our bald-headed residents still lingering over his coffee and dessert at a nearby table.

"Hey, what the hell——" he yelled. We couldn't believe our eyes. Beautiful smiling Vera was hanging over the balcony rail above, pouring her hot coffee on the shocked and scalded resident.

I shouted, "Oh, no, Vera! Stop!. Please stop!" But that wasn't all. Vera had stripped off all her clothes. I sprinted up the stairs to the balcony, peeling off my sweater to cover her, while Ed limped along behind me.

I was recalling my earlier discussion with Sharon Kingsley and her mother in the office. She had assured me that her mother was just "very shy" when I had noted that she appeared to be somewhat sedated during the interview.

Why hadn't I listened to my intuitive feelings and waited for a detailed medical report? But Vera had been such an appealing and attractive lady during the interview, and her daughter was so enthusiastic about the Lingerwood facilities. Not only that, it was a part of our job to see that all apartments were kept rented.

We hustled Vera back to her apartment, talking to her like a child, and assuring her that everything would be fine. She seemed confused at our sudden wild activity, but calmed down when we urged her to take a nap, telling her we would check in with her later in the day.

Vera's stay with us would be quite short, as her behavior became more and more bizarre, especially when she soon became enamored of randy Bud Willful, the resident next door to her apartment. But that's another story.

After the noon meal most of the residents went to their apartments to watch TV, read or nap. Ed drove the residence bus for those wanting to go shopping or to doctor appointments. Now, with a little peace and quiet I figured maybe I could get the newsletter finished, start on the record-keeping, and return phone calls.

It was a lost cause.

My God, what was that? A deafening bang-bang, ding-ding echoed throughout the huge building. It was the general whole building fire alarm. I felt as though someone had crashed two cymbals together in my brain. When it went off, all of the huge hall doors automatically slammed shut, sealing off both three-story apartment wings from the rest of the building.

Now I dialed 911 for the third time of the day, but I needn't have. I already heard sirens screaming as they drove up, followed by paramedics. One of the residents had put a couple of rice cakes in her toaster-oven, discovering too late that they are very inflammable when it was turned on "high." She had called in the emergency. There were red faces, apologies and sighs of relief as shattered nerves and elevated blood pressures again tried to return to normal.

I was beginning to understand why there had been a turnover of *seven* co-manager couples in the past year. Already I felt like quitting. At the very least, I needed a vacation after just six days. My head pounded. Maybe this was some kind of an initiation and everything had been staged just to see what our reactions would be. Maybe we were in some kind of a new TV show called "The Crazy-Makers." But it was all too real. We both continually reminded ourselves on how lucky we were to find a job anywhere, where our ages were supposedly an asset, not a liability.

The Lingerwood bus which Ed was driving arrived back just as the fire engines were leaving. The passengers, hearing about the fire, were reassured that no harm was done except to the rice cakes and the toaster.

"Oh, but that's not all," Ed rather sheepishly reported to me. "I left with eleven passengers and came back with ten."

I felt a fist in the pit of my stomach opening and closing. "We won't have a chance to quit this job. We'll be fired," I muttered Though this was supposedly an ambulatory facility, a few residents still drove their own cars. I recruited one of them to go to the Mall and help find lost Maude. George, a retired surgeon, volunteered. He would drop Ed off at the clinic to check on the healing of his banged-up knee, and go back to the Mall in search of our missing lady.

Less than five minutes later, a Yellow Cab cruised up to the door. Out staggered Maude, mad as that proverbial wet hen. Shaking a fist at me she screeched, "That husband of yours is an idiot. He drove right off without me when he knew I was waiting for him." She claimed that she stood and waited right where Ed had promised to pick her up and he then deliberately went off and left her. Actually she had become confused and had gone out the wrong door and had waited at the wrong side of J. C. Penney's. Scowling angrily, she wobbled past me, aiming for the front door.

Ed and George soon returned, with Ed dazed and glassy-eyed from pain, frustration and lack of sleep. He stumbled through the lobby and to bed for a rest.

I heaved an exasperated sigh and returned to the office to find a startling visitor interested in a vacant apartment. It wasn't her bright orange hair, oversized hoop earrings and tortoise-shell lorgnette that stunned me as much as the large parrot perched on her shoulder. It took me a few seconds to recover my composure. "Well, hello," I said, distracted by the colorful bird now eyeing me malevolently. "I'm Jackie Hibler. How may I help you?"

She replied with a thick Hungarian or Rumanian accent, and I had to concentrate to understand her Za-za lilt. She introduced herself as Madame Lara Crudescu, and said she had been an entertainer and singer in her younger years, traveling all over the Continent. She asked to see an apartment. As we made our way down a residential hall, she commented, "Ah, Jack-ee, I zee you have many splendid paintings and prints, all copies, of course. I have seen ze originals in ze finest palaces and homes of Europe."

I tried to walk close enough to hear what the Madame was saying and still stay far enough away from the sharp beak and claws of her feathered shoulder piece. The lady was obviously impressed with the beautiful art objects, furnishings, and paintings decorating the halls, game rooms and lounges. The parrot with its brilliant plumage, eyed me with suspicion and gutteral squawks.

We stopped at the door of the available two-bedroom apartment and I unlocked the door. "This is one of our nicer apartments. You will notice that it is near the elevator and just down the hall from another lounge area," I explained.

After walking through the apartment she noted that this one did not have an outside balcony. "Oh, but Jack-ee, I must have a balcony for my Count Dracula!"

I eyed the colorful bird with new interest.

"Count Dracula?" I commented. "What a dramatic name for a bird."

"Ah, yes," she said with a mischievous smile. "He came from Transylvania and has been my closest companion for 30 years. But, no, I am sorry. He must have his balcony and railing for his rest."

Suddenly she halted and turned to me with another questioning smile. "Oh, Jack-ee," she lilted, " You must tell me; you like good joke?"

I assured her I did, not knowing quite what to expect.

"You know, I was very close to royal families when I lived in both Romania and Hungary. Do you remember young King Carol of Romania? That was back in the thirties. He was dear friend of mine, as was his young lover, Magda Lupescu."

She paused for a moment, and asked me, "You have heard funny limerick about King Carol and Magda, no?"

I said I vaguely remembered the names, but hadn't heard the limerick.

Quoted Lara, with elaborate theatrical gestures, "There once vas a woman named Lupescu, who came to King Carol's rescue. Said Magda, 'It's a vonderful thing to be under a king, so vy a republic, I esk you?' "

My new acquaintance screeched with raucous laughter, and Dracula joined in with squawks and flapping wings. He also made a small deposit on her shoulder.

Suddenly doors up and down the hallway opened gingerly, as napping residents, awakened by all the Balkan revelry, peered out to see what the squawking and laughter was about.

Lara Crudescu didn't get her apartment, but as they left, I swore the evil bird squawked an obscenity at me. Maybe it was just its Transylvanian accent.

Coffee service was slow during supper but no one seemed to mind while Ed played the concert grand piano for diners. Everyone was happy to see Mazie-mouse, pace-maker now at full voltage, returning in time for supper, looking and sounding chipper as ever. Just one more bizarre day.

. . . And That Lingerwood Conference

At 8:00 p. m. the next evening three teen-age boys and three girls, summer kitchen and dining room staff, came in for their dreaded conference. They looked solemn in their black slacks, white shirts with black bow-ties. Their apprehension and irritation for being kept after their work day was very apparent.

I covered the "fooling around in the pantry" episode quickly by mentioning professionalism, wanting a good reference for a better job in the future and the old saying, "there's a time and place for everything." As for rude and impatient behavior toward the guests, that was a different matter.

I discussed and explained "empathy."

"This is what we need to feel for these people we serve." I pointed out that residents had all suffered losses: loss of a spouse in most cases, loss of independence when they had to give up their cars, loss of their home and familiar surroundings. Many had moved here only as a convenience for surviving relatives, or for their children and grandchildren who visit them. Others here really have no one even to care about them. Everything here is new and different, often frightening. The women are usually able to adjust far more easily than the men."

My restless listeners just averted their eyes, coughed impatiently and shuffled their feet.

"So many times you may feel that they're crabby and unreasonable," I went on. "But if you can remember that many of these old dears also suffer from chronic pain it should make it easier for you to be patient and understanding. They really love seeing your fresh young faces; but you also remind them of how old they are. If you can smile, give them a gentle touch on a shoulder or a pat on their hand and tell them how much you miss your own grandparents, or make some other appropriate comment, it can change the mood dramatically.

"When you have succeeded at this job," I continued, "you will have learned one of life's greatest lessons—how to get along with people." I gave them all a hug and sent them on their way.

I then made one last attempt to finish my newsletter and record-keeping before closing the office at ten o'clock. Ed came in, and limped around to all the doors for a last security check before falling into bed.

Two hours later we were awakened, again out of a dead sleep, to a persistent banging and rattling, seeming to come from the front door. Harry (Bud) Willful, the facility's 85-year-old resident lothario and lady-killer, was home from his weekly downtown seniors' dance. Typically, he had forgotten his key. I put on my robe, wobbled to the door, let him in, then crawled back into bed.

Ed reached out for my hand, and said, "I'm really sorry, honey."

"Sorry?" I asked.

"Yeah," he murmured, "for getting you into this mess."

"It's okay;" I whispered. "Didn't someone once say, "there are no bad experiences, only good material for a book.?' "

Ed reports. . .

The Trouble With Ernie

For a week or so, amazingly, things at Lingerwood went fairly smoothly. Routine days with routine events, no 911 calls, no paramedics. We even had a special fashion show for the women put on by a local theater group. It all went beautifully, with a nice luncheon and tea co-sponsored by a nearby women's organization.

But still no report or word from our managers still back in Michigan with their family emergency. Suddenly, the spell was broken.

Jackie and I had just opened the office one morning when Ernie Jorgenson, one of our oldest residents, shuffled in, shaking his head in seeming confusion.

"Good morning, Ernie," we chorused. "You seem upset. What can we do for you?"

Ernie again shook his head and kept rasping, "I can't wake her up, she won't wake up. . .I don't know what to do."

"Ernie," I interrupted, "are you talking about Edie?" Edie was his wife of some 60 years.

He nodded and kept repeating "I can't wake her up."

Jackie and I grabbed a pass key and went with Ernie up to his second-floor apartment. On opening the door it was immediately apparent that Edie had died during the night, and that her body had slipped half off the bed onto the floor.

We gently lifted her back to the bed. Ernie collapsed into a chair near the bed, sobbing quietly as ambulance attendants arrived and took Edie to a local funeral home. She was 86 years old. She and Ernie had been married 61 years with five children, and, Ernie told us later, they had twelve grandchildren and five great-grandchildren. Edie had gone peacefully and quietly into the night, with Ernie right at her side.

But this wasn't the end of a sad event. Two days later, Henry Jorgenson, one of Ernie's sons from out of state, came to Lingerwood to check on what had happened to his mother, and to help arrange for the funeral. He was a stocky intense man in his late forties and obviously impatient.

Ernie was out of the facility at that moment, visiting with local friends who had come to get him away temporarily from the sad scene. We told Henry about the circumstances of his mother's death, but he seemed irritated and impatient with us. When we told him that his mother had been taken to the Wellflauer Funeral Home, he snapped, "Why wasn't I notified about this earlier?"

We explained that there had been very little time to cope with the emergency of her death. Not only that, we told him, we had no record of the addresses or phone numbers of any of Ernie's children. It apparently had been an oversight when they first registered with Lingerwood, long before we arrived on the scene.

"Outrageous, simply outrageous! You people are totally incompetent!" stormed Henry. We gave him the address of the Wellflauer Funeral Home and he turned and bolted out the office door.

Both Jackie and I looked at one another and shook our heads. "Well, thank heaven that's over," I said. Only it wasn't.

In less than half an hour the phone rang and it was Henry, seething on the phone. "I'm going to sue you people, you idiots," he ranted. "My mother is not here and they don't know why you sent me to this place to find her. Where are you hiding my mother? What are you people covering up? Now *where is she*?" he roared irrationally.

I could only tell him that The Wellflauer Home was where we were told she was taken, and said I would call the ambulance service and find out what their records showed.

I called and discovered that Edie had been taken to the Bellflower Funeral Home on the other side of town. Wellflauer and Bellflower, a total alliterative snafu.

In any event, Henry finally made contact with Bellflower, the funeral was held, Henry didn't sue us, and that wild and weird happening was soon eclipsed by other events.

Jackie reports. . .

Pearl Reveals a Gem

One afternoon 90-year-old Pearl, our ascerbic lady who constantly tattled on others at Lingerwood and periodically accused staff members of sneaking into her apartment and stealing her underwear, came in to the office, shuffled over to my side of the desk, grabbed my shoulder, and with piercing watery eyes, hissed,

"Do you know what's been going on up there on the second floor?" She looked furtively back over a shoulder to see who might be listening.

I pushed myself away from the desk and her bony hand and shook my head.

"No, what's been going on?" I asked. I wondered what kind of a story she was conjuring up this time.

"Well, it's that Bud—or Harry— Willful—you know who he is—has been sparking that crazy woman, Vera. She's right next door to him, you know. And she's right across the hall from me."

"Sparking her?"

"Well, he's probably doing a lot more than just sparking. He's in her apartment night after night." Her face twisted into pure outrage. "One night Vera came out into the hall with this silly look on her face, and had just a filmy nightie on, with Bud in his pajamas stumbling along right behind her. He caught up with her and started pawing her, and, well— then Vera just giggled at it all. But, oh, I tell you, it was just awful." Pearl kept shaking her head in obvious disgust.

"You're not making this up?" I asked her.

"No, no, no! They've been playing these games now for more than a week," she rasped. "Everybody's talking about it." She turned and thrust her wrinkled face into mine and demanded, "What are you people here going to do about it?"

"Pearl," I assured her quietly, "We will have a talk with both Bud and Vera, and see what the real story is."

"You better do more than talk. This is sinful. Scandalous! And right next to my apartment. I don't think people outside this place will appreciate hearing that Lingerwood is becoming a bordello."

Bordello? Lingerwood? The whole idea was ludicrous. But such a story really could cause us a lot of trouble if it got blown up out of proportion, and we had to figure out how best to handle such a mess. Indeed, we first needed to find out if Pearl's story was true, or was itself blown up from observing innocent geriatric flirting.

After all, her stories of underwear and other thefts had proved to be a combination of bad memory and a paranoid personality.

Bud did have indeed a reputation of being a ladies' man, especially from stories we got which filtered back from his weekly attendance at his seniors' dance group in town. A huge barrel of a man, now in his late 70s, he had been married five times, fathered at least eight known children, and was reported to have had a number of other liasons in earlier years. If he still had that randy fire going, we'd have to find some way of cooling it down or request him to find other accommodations.

But Vera, already a behavioral problem, would also probably have to be moved to some other more therapeutic facility if and when we could contact her daughter, now traveling in China. We decided to contact big brash Bud first.

Both of us knocked on his door late the next afternoon. He answered the knock with a hearty "Yo," and opened it to reveal himself in underwear and sheepskin slippers, with the TV roaring in the background.

"C'mon in," he bellowed, and for the first time we noticed that he was nearly stone deaf without his hearing aid. He didn't seem to mind receiving us in his nearly altogether, and motioned for us to sit down. His apartment was amazingly well ordered, and clean.

"Hey, folks, what can I do for you? Like a beer?" he asked with a big Scandanavian smile. "Haven't seen you up here in my neck of the woods since I came here. Really a nice place, Lingerwood. Like it here. Good people, good food, and friendly ladies. I like that," he smiled with a subdued Swedish chuckle.

"And that's what we'd like to talk with you about, Bud," I said. "I don't quite know how to put this to you, but some of the other folks here are upset over what they think is going on with you and Vera. I . . ." Bud interrupted me with a huge bellowing laugh.

"They're upset? Now ain't that a caution! And just what is it they say's going on? And who says?" He looked at us both with an amused grin and rocked back in his big chair, seeming to enjoy the whole conversation.

Ed chimed in and said, "Well, Bud, we hear that you and Vera have a pretty lively relationship going on here, one that's not very private, apparently. One of your neighbors tells us that she's seen you, as she put it, 'pawing' Vera right out in the open, and in the middle of the night."

Bud tilted his head back and nearly collapsed with laughter at that remark, slapping both knees and hooting like a crazy owl. When he got control he said,

"Yah, she's pretty good paw, all right, but a nice lady, too. We're good friends and I try to keep her entertained. She's really a very upset woman, you know. I think I'm helping her cope with a whole new life here. She seems to like me, and who'nell's business what we do, anyway? We're not hurting anyone." He was suddenly frowning.

"I'll bet it was that old crone, Pearl, who's stirring this up. Damn bitch, she is."

I looked at Ed, and he at me, and we nodded towards the door to each other and got up to leave.

"Well, Bud," I said, "you're a lively guy and an attractive man. . ." Here he interrrupted me with an elborate bow, saying, "Why, thank you, Jackie. You're not bad yourself, you know!"

I ignored that remark and continued toward the door, saying, "No one is really trying to interfere in your private life, Bud. It's just that Vera, attractive though she is, has become a real behavioral problem for us here for reasons she can no longer control. As soon as it can be arranged we will help her find more suitable accommodations where she can get the help and treatment she needs."

Ed joined me at the door and, looking back into the room at big bad Bud, he said. "You're a good man, Bud. But just remember that with Vera you're dealing with a woman who is no longer completely in control of herself and her thinking. Please help us to take care of her while she's still with us. Just take it easy with her. Comfort her; be a friend to her. But please try not to get too emotionally involved—for her sake—and for yours, too."

Bud, by now more subdued, just nodded. "Okay, yah, will do," he said as we closed his door.

On the way down to the office in the elevator, prickly Pearl joined us. "'Howdy, Pearl, " Ed said cheerfully. "Seen anyone else sparking things up recently?" He was kidding, but Pearl just glared and knocked him in the shins with her cane as they left the elevator.

Case closed, we hoped.

Ed reports. . .

The Day Hot Air Failed

California's North Bay area is justly famed for its natural beauty, endless rows of wine grapes, sophisticated wineries, and its daily flights of colorful hot air balloons. Whenever days were filled with warm sun and calm air, dozens of these large balloons would take to the air, passenger baskets filled with tourists for a swing across the local Valley and spectacular views of one of the world's great wine-growing areas.

One warm August morning I was out in front of the Lingerwood Residence doing my thing with the rose garden and occasionally glanced up at several of these brilliantly colored balloons, looking like enormous Easter eggs as they floated gently overhead. I could hear the occasional blasts from their flaming propane hot air generators, and noted one in particular, much lower than the others, drifting directly towards our building as it continued to lose altitude.

In less than a minute I could hear the two passengers in the cargo basket and their guide shouting back and forth, with the guide frantically trying to get his burner reignited so that fresh hot air would give him altitude. Nothing seemed to work.

Suddenly, in a light breeze, as the big envelope swept across the meadow directly across from Lingerwood less than a hundred yards from where I stood, the guide saw me and shouted, "Call the fire department—quick. I think we're going to crash!"

At that very moment a grocery delivery truck drove into the scene and inexplicably ran off the road and crashed into a telephone pole next to our building. The driver apparently had been watching the crashing balloon and not the road.

The truck immediately caught fire, and the driver rolled out of his door onto the pavement to safety.

I dashed into the office, made the call, then ran back outside to see what I could do to help. The balloon by now had slowly and steadily swept lower and lower until it was scarceful ten feet off the ground. It's basket and passengers finally bounced into the turf adjoining our rose garden, skipped over the burning truck and its panicked driver, bounced again—hard, and dumped all three people onto the ground. The young man and woman tumbled into the thorny roses; their guide went overboard with a somersault onto the lawn. All three were yelling. A puff of wind then rolled the collapsing envelope and crumpled basket past our building onto the parking lot where it settled over several cars as its remaining warm air escaped.

At this point fire engines with screaming sirens roared up. The firemen immediately doused the truck fire and checked the bruised driver while I ran over to the two balloon passengers, neither of whom seemed to be hurt. Their guide was already on his feet brushing himself off. "Jeez," he kept saying shaking his head. "Jeez. They'll fire me."

"Some honeymoon," said the young man. He and his battered bride both sat up and shakily brushed themselves off. They watched as their shaken guide frantically tried to pull the balloon's envelope off the parked cars.

By now virtually everyone in the Lingerwood building was either hanging out of a window or out on the lawn watching all the excitement. Then, Herb Maillard, one of our newer but older residents, ran over towards me and the two passengers, and suddenly clutched his chest, keeled over, and passed out.

This time we didn't need to call the paramedics. They were right there, less than ten feet from Herb. In seconds they had an oxygen mask on his face and were lifting him into their ambulance which had arrived with the fire engine.

The rest of the engine crew, making sure that there was no further danger of fire from the balloon's propane hot air generator, checked over the two shaken passengers, and found them okay, though in shock from their brush with disaster.

Ken Rudolph, one of the firemen, by now familiar with me after their repeated calls at Lingerwood, came over to me and said wryly, "Ed, don't you guys at this place have anything else to do? Gadfry, what a joint!"

He and the rest of his crew immediately took off behind the ambulance headed for another emergency call.

A check with the hospital told us that Herb was okay after his bout with heart arrythmia, but he remained overnight for a check-up before coming back to his apartment with us.

Ken was right. Gadfry, what a joint.

Jackie reports. . .

Water, Water Everywhere

Shortly after the hot air balloon episode a new mess appeared that momentarily seemed to dwarf that problem with the Titanic.

Once again Ed and I were awakened in the early hours of the morning with that clang-clang of the building fire alarm, and the thudding crash of the huge automatic hall doors in each wing.

We flopped out of bed into our robes and slippers and panic-waddled down to the office to see what had triggered this emergency. I looked at my watch. Three-thirty. Yet no room alarm showed on the office emergency panel. We shut off the alarm din and decided to check out each floor to see if we could find a problem somewhere.

The dining room, music room and games room seemed clear. So was the kitchen. On the second floor we found nothing, either, but ran into several residents awakened by the alarm. We told them it was apparently a false alarm and helped them get calmed down and back into bed.

The third floor was just as quiet. No smoke, no evidence of anything wrong.

We took the elevator down towards the office for another check. At the second floor the door opened just as the lights and power went out.

Fortunately we always kept a flashlight in the elevator and we were able to get out and stumble our way back down the stairs to the office in pitch blackness. About the only light in the whole building was an emergency wall lamp in the kitchen which came on with batteries whenever power was lost.

We followed the dim reflected light through the big dining room out into the kitchen and then we both heard it. Drip, splash, gurgle, then a steady bong-bong as if water somewhere was pounding the bottom of a kettle or pan .

We frantically went all through the huge kitchen, into the pantries and grocery storage rooms but found nothing. Ping, bong, splash.

The dripping and splashing sounds now seened to be coming from the far end of the dining room in an area we missed en route to the kitchen.

Then we saw it. My flashlight followed what was quickly becoming a steady column of water pouring through the ceiling right over our coffee carafes. Scarcely believing our eyes, we dashed up to the second floor and this time found water flooding out under a resident's door onto the hall carpeting. Ed got out his pass key, banged on the door, and when no one answered, opened it. The whole living room floor of this empty apartment was flooded.

Ed sloshed through to the apartment's kitchen with the flashlight and saw water again coming through the ceiling. We were now directly over our dining room coffee carafes where we had first seen the flood. This meant the leak, or whatever it was, now had to be on the top—the third—floor.

The elevator was out of action so we raced with flopping wet slippers up the stairs to the room where we felt sure we'd finally find the problem. It was the apartment of the McGuires, who had this very day left on a trip to Europe. Ed again opened the door and was aghast to find that they had apparently left a kitchen faucet on with the drain totally clogged. The sink was overflowing and the entire apartment was flooded

Ed shut off the water and we both sloshed our way back to the ground floor in an attempt to find out what had happened to our power and phones. Everything was out. But we needed help—fast.

Ed floundered out the front door to a pay phone at the end of the porch, installed for visitors use, and called the fire department. But this was only the beginning.

Going back into the darkened building we heard shouts and calls all coming to us from this same flooded wing. Then residents began surging out of their apartments and down the stairs with their own flashlights.

They all were shouting at the same time, most of them madder than a bunch of outraged hornets. "What the hell's going on?—my place is flooded." roared one irate resident.

"I think I'm going to faint— our whole closet has collapsed onto the floor. All our clothes are ruined and the ceiling is coming down on us, and we don't have any lights. . . . .My God, what's happened! What are you doing about it. . ." And on and on.

Both Ed and I, now shivering from cold, wetness and fatigue, did our best to calm everyone down and explained that someone on the top floor had absent-mindedly left a faucet on before leaving on a trip, creating the flood. If any of them wished to go to a hotel, Ed would drive them to a nearby motel in the company bus until such time as we could get the mess cleaned up. Half a dozen surly, soggy and outraged residents took up our offer.

Old Red Hartman, the residence's well-named curmudgeon, shook his fist in Ed's flashlight's beam," and screamed, "I'm gonna sue you bastards for everything you've got. You're running a crazy house here." Couldn't argue with that; everyone's in a suing mood these days, I mused.

Ed escaped further verbal abuse by spending the rest of the night running back and forth to a local motel with the bus.

The fire department arrived and helped us begin a cleanup as daylight revealed what a really ghastly mess we had on our hands.

Our power had gone out because the flooding water had shorted out the facility's main electrical panel, and took with it our house telephone connections and elevator power. Subsequent damage: three apartments on all three floors had to be completely refurbished. That meant new wiring, new carpets, new flooring, new wallpaper, new plaster and/or wallboard in walls and ceilings, and virtually all new light fixtures in several rooms. Replacement of damaged furniture in two apartments raised the costs even more. Clothes rods in two closets had collapsed, ruining, as one lady had already wailed, hundreds of dollars worth of clothes and other closet-stored stuff. Add to that costs of motel rooms for half a dozen residents for more than three weeks, brought the total up into many thousands of dollars.

It took a month to get everything back to normal, whatever that was. A report later from company headquarters out of state told us that insurance apparently covered most of the damage and we were not held responnsible. No one gave us any words of encouragement, either.

Herman Pigs Out

Ed reports. . .

Among the first things we had to learn as managers was the general health level of each resident when they registered with us. Though all residents had to be "ambulatory" to be accepted at Lingerwood—meaning that they had to be able to walk to meals—many nevertheless were on some kind of a drug regimen for everything from high blood pressure to stress reduction and/or general pain relief.

Generally, food preparation and presentation at meals was of very high quality. We had a registered dietician on call for special dietary concerns , and we did our best to be aware of eating problems some of our residents might have.

Some of them had physical problems that needed to be carefully monitored. Tattle-tale Pearl had a dairy products allergy; Big Bad Bud had high blood pressure; Maizie had a fluttery heart; crabby old Red Hartman had to be careful about too much coffee. It made him twice as crabby.

But it was Herman Dillworth who became our first dietary disaster. Herman was a cheerful, heavy-set, black-haired back-slapping sort of chap everyone liked. He was full of stories about his earlier life as a Merchant Marine officer, and he just loved to eat, especially desserts.

Wednesday morning was usually our cooks' bakery day, and on this particular day, which also happened to be Herman's 79th birthday, they went all out with three different kinds of cake, four kinds of pies, and other pastry odds and ends like cream puffs and chocolate eclairs.

After an outstanding lunch ("dinner" to the residents) of roast beef, Yorkshire pudding, both mashed and candied sweet potatoes, and several vegetables, the diners stood and applauded as our head chef carried in a huge German chocolate cake with 79 flaming candles aboard, with everyone singing a rousing "Happy Birthday, Herman."

Beaming, Herman gazed expectantly as the chef carved out a huge piece of glistening cake for him, deposited it on a large plate—and then added a big double scoop of vanilla ice cream atop it all.

Herman raised his hands overhead in a self-congratulatory hand-clasp, then dug into the cake. He clearly loved every morsel, and then had two more pieces, plus a piece of both freshly baked apple pie—with ice cream—and a piece of lemon meringue to top it all off.

It took happy Herman about an hour to finish it all. When he had scraped off the last bit of frosting and pie crust from his plate, he wiped his mouth with his napkin, heaved a big satisfied sigh, pushed back from his table, then stood up unsteadily as he thanked all his fellow residents for their birthday singing. He then immediately collapsed unconscious to the floor. Pandemonium broke out in the dining room.

Pearl had been sitting right next to Herman, and screeched "He's dead" and fainted out of her own chair to the floor. Three cooks raced in from the kitchen to find out what all the shouting and screeching was about. At least a dozen diners who had remained in the dining room to see Herman's cake presentation, now rushed pell mell either to the elevator or outside. Jackie, who had been pouring coffee at the table next to Herman's, hurried to his side, checked his pulse, then rushed into the office to call our familiar 911.

I first busied myself with trying to get Pearl back to consciousness. Once she regained her wits I helped her back to her chair, and then back up to her room. Paramedics reached Herman in less than ten minutes and he was off to the nearby hospital, sirens screaming all the way. The dining room gradually returned to its peaceful demeanor.

We had assumed that Herman had had a heart attack, but that was not the case. The hospital reported that he had dropped into a diabetic coma—he apparently was an undisclosed diabetic and had not told us of the condition when he registereed with us. He apparently had been attempting to control the condition with just diet—no insulin shots, and it had seemingly worked—up to the time of his birthday sugar-eating orgy.

We immediately notified his daughter, Jennifer, who lived locally, that he had been hospitalized. Our records showed that she had been with Herman when he had registered. However, in reviewing his medical history neither of them had mentioned a diabetic condition to us.

After visiting her father in the hospital, who by now was beginning to come out of his near-death coma, Jennifer, a big bombastic 50-ish brunette, came storming into our office yelling that she was going "to sue this place for everything you have." We were clearly at fault and disgracefully neglectful , she stormed, for not "keeping her father on his diet." Here we go again, I thought. Another lawsuit.

Of course we pointed out to her that neither Herman nor she had advised us of his medical condition, or that he had any dietary problem of any kind. Not only that, we said, common sense would indicate that any person should be aware of his own medical needs, and that included being careful of what he eats.. We clearly were not liable, and referred her to our legal department if she really wished to follow through with her threats.

She grabbed her purse off Jackie's desk and stormed out of the office as fast as she had come in. We never heard another word from her—and Herman, her father, made a complete recovery and was back with us in a few days, now being very careful of what he was eating—and also on a new insulin injection regime.

Lucie's Truthful Fantasy

Jackie reports. . .

One lady at Lingerwood will forever be in our memory. Lucie Harrison had become the facility's resident poet and story-teller. In fact at age 88 she already had had half a dozen or her books of light-hearted poetry published, and was writing another, based on her experiences at Lingerwood.

Lucie was an elegant distinguished looking woman with a perpetual cheerful smile wreathed with a silver halo of carefully coiffed hair. She and husband Bob, a tall but stooped long- retired military officer, now well past ninety, shared a lovely two-bedroom apartment. Both of them were popular with the other residents who often competed to get them to share their dining room tables. But talented Lucie had one very serious problem.

She was 98% blind, a victim of macular degeneration, a severe and incurable retinal condition. Not only that, she stubbornly refused to admit she couldn't see most things around her, except for a tiny patch of light in the outskirts of her visual field.

Lucie was an early riser and, out of necessity so was I. It was thus on one particular morning I went to check on our kitchen crew, and to see that service doors were unlocked and ready for delivery of food supplies, and coffee pots turned on. The smell of coffee was soon wafting throughout the building and I shortly heard the familiar tap-tap of Lucie's cane as she came down the hall and knocked on my office door, opening it with a, "Yoo hoo, it's Lucie.'"

I had a report to finish before breakfast was served, so I didn't look up, but answered," Sit down, Lucie; I'm nearly through with this report, then we'll have time for a quick chat before breakfast."

I had always admired Lucie's wonderful sense of humor and clever rhymes, so working with her and typing her hand-printed work was a task I thoroughly enjoyed. Because of her failing eyesight she had to use a super-sized magic marker on large sheets of paper to write her poetry.

I now turned towards her, saying, "There, I'm finished at last. Okay, Lucie, let me see what you have for me today." I looked up as she handed me a sheaf of boldly printed papers. But this morning there was something very odd about her. I found myself staring at her, then realized what it was that made her look so strange.

A few days earlier we had had a cosmetic "make-up" demonstration that Lucie had enthusiastically attended. The ladies were all encouraged to use eyebrow and lip pencils in applying their make up. Today, incredibly, Lucie had mixed hers up, producing lush blue-brown lips and flaming scarlet eyebrows.

Lucie giggled just as hard as I did when I told her what she had done. She began singing "Bring on the Clowns," as I was gently reversing her bizarre make up.

What a delight this dear lady was! She made up for all our

Lingerwood complainers and whiners. Lucie even referred to them as the "Grumble Bees" in a typically poetic effort. Just a few lines from her whimsical doggerel:

GRUMBLE BEES

I've uncovered one thing
    Down through the years,
Some folks are hard to please.
    So, inventing a name
For these chronic complainers,
    I'll call them "Grumble Bees."
When people are young,
    They want to be old;
Dieters all seem
    In a class by themselves,
I hardly know where to begin,
    The thin ones stuff,
Much more than enough,
    And the fat ones starve to be thin.
And blondes and brunettes,
    Are continually swapping,
The color of each other's hair. . .

One day Lucie and I were chatting over a pot of tea in one of the rare times I ever had to sit and relax for a moment. We had been at Lingerwood now not quite three months, and I was sort of summarizing some of the amazing experiences we had had in just that short time. While Lucie listened I noted that she also was jotting notes on a large piece of paper with one of her giant felt pens.

"What're you doing there, Lucie?"

"Nothing special; just had a few ideas I wanted to jot down. A lot of the things you've been talking about here I think should get written up."

She folded up her paper, gave me a hug and tap-tapped her way back down the hall to her apartment. Late that afternoon she was back in the office with a whole sheaf of new papers for me to type for her.

I was astounded to see what she had written in less than four hours, all taken from our talk together:

How Do Managers Manage?
by Lucie Harrison

It's a new position,and you're on exhibition,
For you stand on full display.
You sometimes wonder why you didn't go under
At the start of that very first day.
In the early morn, at the crack of dawn,
You see that the coffee is hot.
You may be half-dead, with a pain in your head,
But you must keep filling that pot.
You then try to eat, but you're doomed to defeat;
A resident is most irate.
"The service is bad, with very slow service to date."
You return to your table and hope to be able
At least to finish your meal.
But your hopes go aground when you hear the sound
Of another frantic appeal.
It seems that a leak, in a john, so to speak
Has leaked clear through the floor,
And downstream to the ceiling, big
Sections were peeling, and flooding
Clear under the door.
As your breakfast was stalled,
The plumber was called,
And at last his job was done.
Then there was that warning flash,
When it appeared there'd been a crash,
And your day had barely begun.
So you sit at your seat, at last ready to eat,

When you hear a disturbing sound.
You look for the trouble, and gaze at the rubble
Of broken dishes all around.
With the kitchen crew everything's askew.
Two of the girls on vacation are away;
You blow your mind, for where can you find
Two to fill in for today?
Each day that you face is another rat-race
For your feet hardly touch the ground.
This is the pits, and you're out of your wits
If you stay on this merry-go-round.
Yes, a manager's life if one of strife,
Or it certainly seems that way;
For there's always some jerk
Who wants you to work
Twenty-four hours a day.
Then you finally get to sleep,
But upward you leap
At the sound of the siren's roar.
And it would appear as it comes near
That it's coming right through your door.
But the whole affair proves just a scare,
For everything came out all right.
But in your dazed condition you're in no position
To return to your sleep that night.
So this life, you decide, you just can't abide,
In spite of your many friends.
As the saying goes, and everyone knows
A candle can't be burned at both ends!

As I read through this amazingly creative and spontaneous work—one also cunningly accurate as it depicted our daily Lingerwood lives—I could not help but feel both privileged and saddened to have known Lucie Harrison. Privileged because of our close friendship, and saddened because at age 88 I knew we probably had little time left to enjoy one another's company.

Little did I know at the time that it wouldn't be Lucie who would first break this close relationship, but me.

One morning, late in August I carried a breakfast tray of food to an upstairs resident too ill to come to the dining room. I had taken the stairs rather than the elevator "For the exercise—so I could stay in shape," I had told myself. Near the top of the first flight of stairs, I tripped, barely caught the tray from flying into the air, and in the process felt something pop with sudden sharp pain in my right ankle. After two weeks of steadily increasing pain, I was unable to walk at all.

After several days of innumerable X-rays, MRI and nuclear bone scans and other exotic tests, I was told by one doctor that I could have either Paget's disease (a progressive crippling disease of the bone), or a bone malignancy which might even require amputation, or phlebitis, or a possible stress fracture. Another doctor thought I might have a stress fracture which did not yet appear on X-rays.

"Sometimes a patient can go months walking around on a painful leg only to find out later that he had an undiscovered stress fracture," he explained. "If not treated they can in some cases break clear through and leave you really crippled."

It was the beginning of the end for our Lingerwood-managing experiment.

With this staggering array of medical good cheer to face, late in September we were forced to quit, and use the small amount we had earned in barely four months to pay off nearly $3,000 in medical expenses over and above our quite inadequate hospitalization coverage. We would have to wait until we returned home for more medical tests before I could find out what was really wrong with my painful leg.

CHAPTER 2

A Time of Regretitude
With a Dash of Hollandaise

Ed reports. . .

It was thus with both regret and gratitude, indeed, many mixed feelings that we headed for home, unoccupied for those summer and early fall months we had been at Lingerwood. There was joy at being home, especially with Joan and Bob again helping us readjust. They helped us load our motor home and car, and Bob even drove our car home for us, with Joan following in their; while I drove the motor home.

After unloading and getting settled in again, I was now busy cleaning up the yard, doing routine maintenance on the house, and trying to help Jackie, now wheel-chair bound, with regular treatment follow-ups into Fresno to see several new doctors, all more than 60 miles from home. She continued to have severe pain when she attempted to walk, even with crutches, which had confounded her doctors. Three different specialists had examined her before we had returned home, and no one agreed as to the source of her ankle pain. X-rays showed no observable fracture. Magnetic Resonance Imaging (MRI) and two bone scans showed nothing, either.

Finally, a fourth orthopedic specialist, after another bone scan, spotted a thin hairline fracture that radiated around the end of the tibia—her shin bone. It was very faint and had somehow been missed by other specialists. It was the culprit.

On checking later with her first doctor, he informed her that he had been convinced that she was suffering from a bone malignancy which couldn't yet be seen on X-rays, and felt that the next time he saw her she would probably have had an amputation. He just didn't have the heart to tell her until further tests confirmed his suspicions. We thanked the Lord he had been wrong.

Deja Vu to the Rescue!

In the meantime those relentless real estate obligations, with interest, were continuing to build, totally erasing what small gains we had made with our Lingerwood stint. It was immediately apparent to me that we had to find some immediate way of augmenting our income, or we shortly would once again be even deeper into our debt nightmare, and might even face foreclosure on both of our homes. I had a sudden brainstorm.

I was browsing through our daily newspaper one morning when I noted an ad for a new type of movie-making camera, one which produced both a visual and auditory track, and which used the new VCR tape cartridge instead of film. One day on a trip into Fresno I checked out the store that had run the ad, looked over the new camera and its accompanying recorder, shot a few test shots in the store, and bought it, using my old reliable teachers' credit union to finance it. I was grateful that we had been able to maintain our credit despite our investments disaster.

Years before in my advertising and sales promotion career I had done a lot of work in commercial 16m movie production, and had developed considerable knowledge and skill in the field. I had shot weddings, commercial assignments for our local community chest fund-raising drives, and other movie programs for business. I knew that I could provide the same services with this new movie medium. It was instantaneous, required no waiting for film development, could be edited right in the camera, and was amazingly low in cost.

I could see opportunities around us everywhere, and began calling on prospects for what we dubbed *Deja Vu Productions*. On our business letterhead and cards we used a cartoon of an elephant's head with the logo, "Deja Vu Never Forgets."

I set about drumming up a new business . I covered a number of weddings and business projects, including a promotional tape for our local Oakhurst Chamber of Commerce. I produced another for a chain of motels in the Yosemite area, copies of which were sent to European travel agents for sales promotion for our local tourism business. Another project was to cover a large convention in Yosemite Valley for a hospital association of some 300 people. But our biggest job was to cover a series of baby beauty pageant programs of the type which had starred little Jon Benet Ramsey of Colorado, later murdered by an unknown killer.

As a retired psychologist, covering these programs was lucrative for us—we sold video copies of the whole progam to parents—but also was an eye-opener into the unconsciously and amazingly egocentric parents of these little tykes. Children scarcely old enough to walk were all gussied up in ridiculous costumes by their mothers, who also had paid a stiff fee to get their kids into the show. And the programs were so rigged that virtually every youngster was some kind of a prize winner, a sure come-on for the next such program..

Some mothers, sitting out in the audience, would go through wild pantomimes as their kids appeared on stage, trying to get them to smile, or to assume some sort of bodily contortion they thought was "cute" and which would appeal to the "judges." Most such motherly entreaties frequently turned into unexpected and embarrassing antics by their kids, all of which we recorded on our master tapes.

I remember in particular one little boy, about five, who hesitantly came out into the glare of the stage lights as his mother out in the audience frantically tried to get him to smile. She put her fingers in both sides of her mouth and stretrched her face into a grotesque mask. The child dutifully put his own fingers in his mouth and did a great imitation of his mother, which unexpectedly brought down the house. I think his mother fainted.

In looking back on these experiences, some of them were fun. But both Jackie and I sometimes shook our heads at the really incredible vanity shown by some of these mothers who were willing to put their tiny children through what often were clearly emotionally upsetting experiences, just to boost their own motherly egos.

But this new business, which had taken off so quickly, and which had temporarily kept our financial heads above water, very soon began to fade. The video equipment I had bought had consisted of two units, one a camera, the other a quite heavy recorder which I carried over a shoulder. Now suddenly on the market came a new video wrinkle, the "camcorder." This combined the camera and recorder in one handy portable unit, was infinitely smaller than my equipment, and was low enough in price to appeal to the mass market. Now everyone could shoot his own home movies, weddings, meetings, conferences. I was virtually out of business. My "clientele" income had faded away, a victim of electronic progress, much like the old 8mm home movie genre.

But in the nearly a year we had been "Deja Vu," we had made over ten thousand dollars. That wasn't a lot of money, but it kept that foreclosing wolf from the door as Jackie's leg finally was healing.

After the months through that winter and spring of two separate casts, plus a walking cast,and physical therapy, she finally reached the point where she could walk with a cane and a walking cast without much pain. By May, despite still having her leg still in that walking cast, she felt strong enough to try for another interview. This one was one of two more referrals from Joan and Bob, asking for a "mature couple to care for a substantial estate."

We called the advertising party on the first referral, gave the lady answering our call a quick resume of our experience and backgrounds, and made an appointment to come for an interview the following Monday afternoon.

Both of us were still leery of trying to get back into a work schedule with Jackie's leg still not fully healed, but with the steadily increasing pressures of mortgage debt piling up on our unsold house, we felt that it was time to try again.

After a 180-mile drive across the great Central Valley, we found ourselves surrounded by posh homes on all sides in a very exclusive section of the lower San Francisco peninsula known as Hillsdale.

We drove our drab little Datsun into a long circular driveway fronting a very large three-story French provincial style home, parked near the three-car garage, noting as we passed, a Rolls-Royce sedan and Mercedes convertible. We walked to the front door and rang the bell. There were the sounds of some shuffling around and the barking of dogs inside the house before a very large but distinguished and pleasant-looking woman answered the door.

We introduced ourselves, shook hands, and she identified herself in a pronounced Dutch or German accent, as Mrs. Van Horst. With a grand smile and sweeping gesture, she invited us in. We were sure we had made a striking impression on our arrival, with a dusty battered car, and Jackie hobbling along with a slacks-covered cast.

Once we were inside it became immediately apparent that this home was a wealthy European expatriate's American transplant from the old country. We were ushered into a high-ceilinged, heavily draped living room furnished with exquisite European antiques; many of the pieces I guessed were from Holland or France. Suddenly two tiny but noisy barking dogs raced into the room and stood in front of us barking incessantly until our hostess called in a young girl, apparently a maid, to take them out

"Ah, those are my children," Mrs. Van Horst laughed. "Oh, they are naughty, naughty, aren't they? Oh, Ja, they are both quite rare pedigreed animals. One, the brown one, is a Brussels Griffon, while the white long-haired one is a King Charles spaniel. And I have another one at the veterinarian's hospital now having her toenails trimmed. She is a French Papillon."

I remembered seeing one of those odd creatures once at a dog show. The name comes from the French word for butterfly, but it is a truly weird and delicate looking small animal with a pointed muzzle, short head, and a long stringy coat. Sort of like a bloated long-haired Chihuahua. I recalled that the breed was a favorite of the medieval French royal Court.

I love dogs, but already I was becoming uneasy in what was appearing to be a glorified European museum populated by weird animals and a large lady of the house who seemed lost in her own effete toys. I glanced at Jackie as the lady recounted all the dreadful problems she had had in finding such rare animals. Jackie's eyebrows went up and down a couple of times. I nodded imperceptibly.

Mrs. Van Horst, a six-foot woman with a cherubic face and a pile of snow white neatly coiffed hair, weighing at least 200 pounds, rose, saying "Perhaps you'd like to see the rest of our home. My husband is presently in Holland, and he is rarely here. Come, let us go upstairs to our bedrooms."

Climbing stairs is not a task easily accomplished by anyone in a leg cast, but Jackie gamely hobbled her way up the impressive wide curving stairs holding on to my arm as the grand lady steamed her way to the second floor.

The house's seven bedrooms were enormous, with walk-in closets large enough to contain not only clothes but also fine museum-piece paintings adorning their walls. Each bedroom's adjoining bath contained that standard European fixture, a bidet, as well as the other usual American equipment. Heavy drapes covered most windows in every room, keeping the interior of the house shrouded in perpetual gloom.

I was becoming more depressed by the minute, and could hardly wait until our hostess sailed grandly down the sweeping curved staircase to her front hall entryway. We returned to the living room where she asked, noticing Jackie's awkward limp, "Mrs. Hibler, do you really think you would be able to take care of this large house, do my cooking, and take care of my 'children' with your leg in that condition?"

Jackie looked at me, I at her, and she said with a big sigh, "Well, I had hoped to be able to handle things like this after this long recovery from my accident. But perhaps right now this would not be the thing for us to do." Mrs. Van Horst nodded in apparent agreement. We all rose, and we thanked the nice lady for her time, walked back out the front door to our little car, got in and both of us burst into tears. It was a combination of disappointment, fatigue, and also the realization that it wasn't yet time to go back to our joint work.

We drove the long road home in almost silence.

Yet in another month—it was now nearly July—Jackie felt enough better to want to try again. Her cast was now off, most of that persistent pain was gone, and she was doing pretty well without a cane. We answered another of Bob and Joan's referrals, this time again in the Bay Area.

CHAPTER 3

Crepes and Sole, or Life in Lululand

Ed reports. . .

We met in the senior executive's office of a posh retail antique and home furnishing chain. The woman interviewing us—Mrs. Lorene Kandahar, —we later dubbed her Lulu— was the owner. She had been in her own very successful business more than fifty years, though we later learned that in earlier years she had been a reported madam in a local luxurious house of joy.

Her customers of that earlier era were reported to have been from The City's elite, even with some of the local clergy blessing her establishment. Profits from this fleshy endeavor apparently were the foundation of her new retail empire. Which may explain why, in middle life, she suddenly had abandoned Moses and fled to Jesus, ultimately becoming a compulsive philanthropist to local Catholic church causes, and a benighted grande dame in local conservative business circles. All of this meant that by now she had to be close to eighty, though she looked much younger.

Her office where we were interviewed was plastered with pictures of herself with reigning politicians, including one with the governor, and ex-president Ronnie and Nancy. Her huge desk was littered with three phones, pencil cups, and other office detritus; its matching enormous chair looked as if it had come from behind a judge's courtroom bench. A two-foot statue of her new patron, St. Jude, stood impassively in a dark corner, with a second miniature replica under her desk lamp.

Lulu was tiny, scarcely five feet tall, with neatly coiffed snow-white hair, very thick and enormous oversize tortoise-shell glasses, and a tightly laced figure which, with her hair, made her look like an upholstered ice cream cone. We noted that her employees, several of whom came into the office during our visit, seemed to be terrified of her. She seemed a true dominatrix.

She finally closed her office door and ordered that all phone calls be held until she was through talking with us.

After what I thought was a rather cursory review of our resumes, in a piercing, rasping fractured-trombone voice she told us of how much she needed someone just like us. She had no children, she said, and we would be "just like her family." Our joint pay would be $2,000 a month to start, we'd have our own apartment with fireplace, private deck, use of the pool and all her exercise equipment, and on and on. And Jackie would only need to prepare two meals, breakfast and dinner, and all her time during the day would be "free."

I would drive them in their enormous white "stretch" Cadillac limo back and forth to work, do the household shopping, serve meals as a butler, and maintain extensive lawns, gardens, and plantings on the huge hilltop lot. It seemed like a natural. Little did we know.

In the middle of her spiel a tiny bald, owl-like man, nearly as small as she, shuffled in, smoking a huge cigar under heavy horn-rimmed glasses. She introduced him as her husband who was technically retired, but at age 88 still came in with her each day to help at the business. We immediately got a deja vu impression of a shrunken actor, George Burns. Of course he immediately became "Burnsy."

Burnsy blew a cloud of smoke at us, grunted enigmatically a few times, and, after a brief exchange, beckoned for us to ride with him to the house so we could look over where we might be working. Because he couldn't drive, and she had to stay at her business, we took our battered little Datsun to the top of the hills overlooking the Bay.

The property was shielded from the street by thick shrubbery and large trees, with an eight-foot steel fence surrounding the entire three-acre estate. But the view from the opposite west side of the house was stupendous, covering the entire Bay area out beyond the Golden Gate bridge clear to the Farallon Islands on the horizon. Surrounding the house were spacious lawns, a large pool, many ornamental shrubs and an orchard of differing kinds of fruit trees.

The U-shaped house itself was truly magnificent, and furnished with the finest of everything. Nothing had been spared to make the place a splendid showplace of vulgar ostentation.

Burnsy showed us through , shuffling from room to room through a haze of cigar smoke, pointing out the elaborate security systems which ringed the whole area. Lulu's bedroom, the centerpiece of the house, included an enormous custom-made circular bed, a mirrored ceiling, with massive oriental-style dressers and chairs, and a giant television set mounted hidden at the foot of the bed which rose hydraulically at the push of a button. Adjoining her bedroom was a large exercise room with a jacuzzi bath, two stationary bikes, and other weight exercise equipment studding the room. Another large statue of St. Jude brooded in one corner.

However, quarters for their help were sparsely furnished, with a small bedroom, a sitting room with a miniature fireplace and separate small deck, just off the large kitchen complex. The entire house and multi-acre estate was ringed and bugged with every conceivable electronic anti-burglary device. Beepers were needed to open the outer iron gate, secret codes to open the entrance door, and special arming and disarming codes for use once inside. We were told that we could not even open a window for fresh air without punching in a disarming code.

After looking over the area, and being under merciless financial pressure with debt relentlessly accumulating on two homes, after returning home we accepted the job, almost exactly a year after our ill-fated Lingerwood experiences began.

However, because all this occurred early in June, we had already planned, come hell or high water, that we would attend my 50th class reunion at Dartmouth College back in New Hampshire. Because Christy, one of our daughters, had been a flight attendant with United Airlines for many years, she generously provided us with air fares to fly back for the great event before we began our new adventure.

The reunion was a spectacular success, and we were now, back home again, ready, we thought, to leave it once more and tackle a brand new adventure.

Freeway Meltdown

Jackie reports. . .

Our new employer, Mrs. Kandahar, now frequently interrupted our frenetic hours of packing, demanding reassurances that we would be there by 11:00 a. m., and arbitrarily demanding that we should en route "pick up crates of fresh fruit as you come through the Valley. . .so you can make jelly or pies"!

Two days after we returned from the reunion we loaded up our old motor home and the drab but sturdy little Datsun with family pictures, stereo, and clothes. I drove the Datsun, following Ed in the motor home. We expected an uneventful four-hour trip. It became an immediate disaster.

Less than a hundred miles from home, in over 100-degree heat, the engine of the venerable motor home began to buck and snort, and finally died, leaving us stranded on Freeway 99 in California's sizzling Central Valley. After fussing with what appeared to be fuel-line clogging, Ed finally got the monster to stumble into the driveway of some friends who lived close by Modesto, where we spent the night.

Though it was great seeing old friends again whom we had not expected to visit at this time, the pressures and anxiety of just one more headache, this time an automotive one, was beginning to take its toll.

I called our new employers to apologize for being unable to get there when we had said we would. The phone rang, and Lulu answered it with her trademark raspy bellow. She greeted my call with an icy silence, then an incredible complaint:

"Who's going to turn down my bed tonight?" she tromboned. That should have been a tip-off. Then our host's neighboring St. Bernard roared and bellowed all night right under our bedroom window.

The next morning, in the jam-packed Datsun, we groggily headed back to the freeway where we had conked out the night before, leaving the gimpy motor home with its huge personal cargo in the hands of our friends who would take it to their mechanic. We had loaded enough underwear and other personal effects into the tiny car, to tide us over till the motor home was fixed. Probably only a couple of days, we figured. We figured wrong.

We finally arrived at what we came to call "the palace" before nine o'clock,

Our arrival at Lulu's palace was hysterically historical. We immediately inadvertently tripped a burglar alarm resulting in screeching sirens and a roaring visit from the local gendarmerie. Lulu stormed out to our car, and without so much as saying hello or good morning, proceded to bawl us out for causing such an outrageous din.

Then, incredibly, in less than half an hour after our confused arrival, she had demanded that I prepare her usual Sunday crepes for breakfast, to be served by the pool not later than 11:00—and we hadn't yet had the chance to unpack or even go to the bathroom. Maybe she was getting even with us for all that excitement. I wondered.

In the supposedly well-furnished kitchen, I now found only two usable pots or pans, a food-processor with missing parts, a nearly empty refrigerator, a pantry with no basic kitchen supplies, a frayed broom, and virtually no usable cutlery. I reported all this to Lulu, who by this time was out by the pool applying oleagenous tanning lotion all over an amazingly well-preserved eighty-year-old body.

In response, the lady spat out a few unladylike obscenities, declaring that "All that stuff was there before you got here." Apparently the previous help had decided to clean house.

Ignoring Lulu's insulting innuendo, I came up with reasonably good crepes made from questionable flour I found on the bottom of a pantry shelf. They apparently were acceptable, because Lulu bawled for more.

A week passed with our crippled loaded motor home back 140 miles away, still not fixed. Continually rewashing our increasingly threadbare underwear was becoming a chore with no opportunity to buy more. But other things that happened during that first week were mind-numbing.

Ed did a daily delivery and pickup of Lulu and Burnsy in their huge stretch Cadillac limo at their downtown business. He reported that Lulu, in deference to her recent conversion, every morning demanded that he stop en route to the office at a medical center where she was a heavy financial contributor, to pray to St. Jude in the place's chapel. In fact Lulu had, as we soon noted, installed the good saint's replica in a variety of sizes all over the house, from garden size to to prayer beads.

Having gotten a prayerful recharge from the gentle saint, on the rest of the daily trip into the office, she would yell at tin-eared Burnsy in the back seat to change the channel on the limo TV to something else. He'd change it, then she'd bellow for him to change it again. In response he'd blow cigar smoke in her face and turn off his hearing aid..

The third day of our stint with these eccentrics, we were in a supermarket parking lot with the big limo where Ed was doing the grocery shopping. Carrying out several bags, he bumped into another customer in the doorway, excused himself, and continued out to the limo. As he walked around to the driver's seat he found the right rear tire flatter than that proverbial pancake.

After calling road service, with what seemed like a hundred people around gawking at the stretch limo with the dumb driver, we got the tire fixed. Then, on returning to the house, Ed discovered that someone had picked his pocket. His wallet, license, and all our credit cards, including others given us by our new employers for shopping use, were gone. Ah, that "bump" in the market doorway.

Ed, figuring we'd probably be fired for the loss, reported it to Lulu. She stared boggle-eyed at him, shook her head and just walked away into her bedroom. Burnsy just shrugged. "Easy come, easy go," he mumbled sardonically through his perpetual cigar smoke. We never did get those credit cards back and Ed had to go through mind-numbing red tape to get his driver's license renewed.

Ed found taking care of the lawns and shrubbery was hard physical work, but I felt it was a breeze compared to what I faced daily. At 7:00 sharp every morning I awakened Lulu, bringing her her six ounces of prune juice warmed precisely to 90o. Exactly six ounces, no more, no less, and it had to be at precisely the correct temperature.

On our second day at the Palace I faced her incredible lecture on the proper way to make her enormous round bed, with fourteen different sized pillows to be arranged in a precise pattern. If she returned home after work and found one pillow a quarter of an inch out of place, nasty pandemonium reigned.

By this time we began to wonder what had happened to that "you'll be just like my family" line. I found that my "free time" between breakfast and dinner was filled with constant phone calls from Lulu at her office wanting to know what I was doing. She'd screech, "What took you so long to answer the phone?" When I said I was busy cleaning her bedroom, she'd testily reply, "My bedroom's not dirty. If it is, you messed it up, not me." Whenever I didn't answer the phone immediately I got a tongue-lashing about "loyalty and dependability."

One memorable afternoon, after the usual barrage of phone calls, I got a friendly call from Joan and Bob, now also living and working again in a nearby area, wanting to know how we were doing. I mentioned that I had been ordered to prepare a filet of sole dinner, and that Lulu insisted that she didn't want butter used, but she wanted the fish "delicate and brown." Because friend

Joan, Cordon Blu trained, fortunately had the day off, and was experienced in every type of gourmet cooking, she said she'd come on over and give me a hand.

Once she arrived, the two of us put together a great sole dinner. However, I asked how I could get the fish "delicate and brown" without using butter.

"Easy," said Joan. "Lie. Use a little butter anyway, and pepper it with paprika. It'll be golden brown and she'll never know the difference." She then proceded to dredge the fish in its usual butter. We also found what appeared to be paprika in a plastic baggie, and dusted it thoroughly over each filet.

Joan had to get back to her job, and left just before Ed went into town with the limo to fetch Lulu and Burnsy.

Soon dinner was coming along to the point where Ed was ready to serve their highnesses in their palatial TV solarium. I arranged two pieces of nicely browned sole with parsley and accompanying vegetables and pilaf on each plate, and Ed headed for the solarium throne room, towel properly draped over one arm, as he said, the way he'd seen it in the movies.

He later said he kept thinking, "Serve from the left, take away from the right—or is it the other way around? Oh, well—the hell with it. They'll be so absorbed in Dan Rather's deafening TV news (Burnsy had a tin ear) they won't know the difference."

Ed had gotten almost to the solarium door with news anchor Dan booming out of the TV, when I raced out of the kitchen and caught his arm. "Good grief, stop!" I hissed, "don't give them that fish! Gimme." I grabbed both plates off his tray and scampered back to the kitchen. Neither Lulu nor Burnsy, focused on booming Dan, had seen us, and Ed followed me back to the kitchen to see what was wrong.

I whispered to him that I had tasted just a tiny piece of the fish as he was leaving the kitchen, and it nearly melted my mouth. What Joan and I had thought was paprika was *cayenne pepper*.

I frantically tried to swab off the pepper and refry the mess into something recognizable, but it all dissolved into goo. Fortunately I was able to salvage extra pieces I had saved for myself and Ed, while he went out to apologize for the delay in serving dinner.

"What's wrong out there? I'm hungry," growled Lulu.

"Nothing serious," Ed lied. "The sole is taking a little special preparation. I'm sure you'll love it."

And they did. The only compliment, up to this time, either of us ever got from either of them was, "Damn good sole," Lulu said. "Loved it. Proves you don't need butter to get it brown."

Smoke Gets in His Eyes

Jackie continues. . .

The following day I got a morning call from Lulu telling me that she wanted barbecued chicken for dinner, and that she wanted Ed to use her new $1000 barbecue machine to prepare it.

"No sense in having that expensive equipment if you don't use it," she bawled.

Ed had done a lot of barbecuing at home on our own simple round Weber, but this new machine, with all kinds of electronic automatic bells and whistles, might give him pause.

When he came in from working in the yard that afternoon I said, "Lulu just called and she wants barbecued chicken for her dinner tonight. And she wants you to use that big new contraption she's got on the deck outside the kitchen."

"Why me?" Ed asked. "You're the cook."

"I don't know a dumb thing about a barbecue, especially one with all that electronic stuff on it. It's your baby, dear. Better get out there pronto and fire it up."

He muttered something under his breath, but went out to check out the new electronic marvel.

It was now nearly five o'clock, and they wanted dinner at six , so I began to put together the vegetables and dessert, and took out the cut up pieces of two chickens, with some barbecue sauce, out to Ed.

"Here's your stuff, dear," I said, handing him the pan." I looked at the now hot barbacue and mentioned that with all those gadgets he ought to create something fabulous.

"Yeah, it'll be fabulous, all right," he muttered. He put on an apron, and turned to get the chicken under way.

I went back into the kitchen to finish preparing the vegetables and the rest of the dinner. It was now nearly six o'clock.

Suddenly I heard Ed bellow, "Jeez, the whole damn thing's on fire! Jackie, get that kitchen fire extinguisher out here—it's in the broom closet. Quick!"

I raced to the door by the deck and saw clouds of smoke and flames billowing out of the machine, then turned to the broom closet for the extinguisher. I leaped out the door, handing it to Ed. He immediately pulled the ring plug on the gadget and a cloud of white smoke poured out of it all over the flaming chicken and the machine.

"My God, Ed, what happened?" I shouted, as the cremated fowl continued to smoulder and sizzle.

"Damned if I know," he growled. " It just suddenly exploded all over the place. I'm lucky I didn't get cremated myself. Now what the hell do we give their highnesses for dinner?"

I shrugged , then took barbecue tongs and picked off the still sizzling machine all the recognizeable pieces of chicken I could find. I put them back in the same pan , and hurried back into the kitchen.

"Wait here," I said to Ed. "I'll be right back with a solution for this mess. But you'd better clean up that machine before you go to get them."

I went to the sink and, using an emery board, laboriously scraped as much of the char and any fire retardant off the meat as I could, then smeared each piece with an overdose of heavy barbecue sauce. I then reheated the whole mess in the kitchen oven. It looked yucky, but I would tell Lulu and Burnsy that Ed and I had conjured up something really special on their new barbecue, and that I was sure they'd love it.

Ed went out to the limo and fetched the two and, again they

confounded us, after they had had their dinner.

"Ed, you're another Wolfgang Puck. Best damned chicken I ever ate," said Lulu, mumbling through her barbecue sauce. "Gimme me your recipe for that sauce. Damn, that was good. Want to give it to my office help."

Burnsy, nodding in agreement, gummed away on a gooey drumstick, muttering unintelligibly. Some people have neanderthal tastes.

After the first two weeks on the job without a day off, I finally asked what days we could have off.

"Time off?" Lulu snapped. "You'll get time off in December when we go to Switzerland for our lamb embryo injections. There's too much work for you here to take any time off now. Your job is to be here when we need you," she rasped. "When we're gone you can have time off, but you'll still have to be around to take care of Lovable." Lovable was their miserable tiny Yorky who screeched and howled in the back of the limo every time we went around a corner.

But who did this arrogant woman think she was kidding? We were desperate, but not enough to put up with such outrageous, irrational baloney. Quite illegal, too. Shortly thereafter, I answered the kitchen phone and got an anonymous phone call from a man with a thick east-Asian accent who, after asking if we were the madam's new house employees, said, "She is bad woman; get out— now. She is *cray*-zee; she will drive you *cray*-zee, too." He hung up abruptly.

Cray-zee was an understatement. But we still had several weird experiences to go through before we were rid of looney Lulu, or she was rid of us.

Riding High

Jackie reports. . .

After more than two weeks confined in Lulu's palace, one morning I felt restless and depressed enough finally to try and get some exercise. During our employment interview Lulu had mentioned that all of her extensive collection of exercise equipment would be ours to use when she was not there.

I was cleaning her bedroom and bath on this particular morning and noted again that classy-looking electric exercise bike that I had seen on our original tour with Burnsy. It had moving handlebars and adjustable speed controls so that you could control the degree of stretch and speed of the pedals to fit your individual body style.

I put down my cleaning equipment, pulled off my rubber gloves and climbed on the contraption, leaning off to one side trying to read the little instruction panel on the frame. I pushed a button that said "on-off," and it started to move. About this time Lovable trotted into the room and when the pedals began to rotate, she started her unearthly screeching and barking, snapping at my ankles as they went around faster and faster. I desperately looked for the speed control switch, but it was nowhere.

In less than a minute the thing was running away with me, with Lovable snapping and screeching at my feet with every revolution. The handlebars were whipping back and forth and I dared not let go. Not only that, the pedals were now going so fast I couldn't keep my feet on them, so I was being jerked back and forth with the handlebars with my still sore leg being bashed by the flying pedals.

I screamed for Ed who was out somewhere working in the yard. But the machine just kept going faster and faster. The faster it went, the louder I screamed, desperately hanging on to those jerking handlebars.

By now dear lovable was nearly foaming at the mouth with all the wild excitement. She nipped one ankle as it came around, but the pedal knocked her clear across the room, leaving her yowling with pain nearly as loud as I was bellowing for Ed.

He finally heard the commotion and came in to see what was raising all the fuss. At the door of the exercise room he stared unbelievingly as I continued to scream and fight to hang on.

I saw him out of the corner of one eye and yelled, "Shut it off! Shut it off! For God's sake shut the stupid thing off!"

"What the hell are you trying to do, make it fly?" he gasped as he finally got unfrozen from his shock at the scene and gingerly reached between my flying legs to hit the off button. I was saved, but Lovable limped around for a few days.

We never mentioned that wild ride to Lulu or Burnsy. But I sure would like to have seen Lulu on that thing. What a vision. . .

"Here Come de Crack Lord!"

Jackie reports. . .

Later that same week I decided to ride with Ed in the limo to the store for some special shopping. We decided to take a different route to the shopping complex where we usually did our household shopping, just for a change of scenery.

I don't know how we did it, but we soon found ourselves completely out of our usual neighborhood, and approaching one of the city's seediest areas.

We were now on a one-way street which seemed to lead further and further into the city's most decrepit neighborhoods. Not only that, the street was so narrow, with no driveways, there was no way to turn the big stretch around without going clear around the next block.

We drove very slowly, noting that passers-by were beginning to stare at the big white limo that clearly did not belong to anyone in the neighborhood. As Ed turned into a larger street with heavier traffic, half way into the intersection the engine suddenly died. The big stretch just squatted there in the middle of the street.

By now pedestrians and other cars had stopped near us to see what was going on. And then several unsavory-looking characters came up to my side of the limo and knocked on the window. I rolled it down just far enough to ask what they wanted.

One of the men, looking first over his shoulder to see who might be watching, asked me in a thick accent, " Hey, whatcha got in there? How much?"

I shook my head and quickly rolled the window back up. Ed still was grinding away on the stalled engine, cursing quietly.

"Jeez, what a place to stall out! Come on, baby, let's fire up, " he wheedled.

I pushed the electric door lock buttons as more rough looking men were gathering around the limo, and I distinctly heard someone say, "Dey must be from de crack lord uptown."

"Crack lord?" I hissed to Ed. "Did you hear that?"

He nodded, still grinding. "Hey, love, give St. Jude a call. Maybe he can help."

"This isn't funny," I snapped.

"Right. T'ain't funny. But maybe I can get one of these guys to call our road service. . ."

He was interrupted by a shrieking siren as a police car growled up along side to see what the problem was. The officer gave us both a suspicious look, and asked to see our IDs. The crowd around us suddenly evaporated.

"What the devil are you two doing in this part of town? Especially driving a rig like this. Don't you realize you could have been set up big time?" He was a bit irritated.

We both nodded sheepishly and told the officer that we somehow had simply made a wrong turn and had never planned to have had such an expedition.

He didn't write us a ticket, and by now, with the engine being off for several minutes, it amazingly started. It probably had simply flooded.

The officer gave us directions on how to get back to where we thought we had been going, and wished us well. I noted him our mirror as we were leaving. He was just shaking his head. We got out of there—fast.

Fun in Burnsy's Boudoir

Jackie reports. . .

During our third week in Lululand, it had been unusually hot and humid during one night. Neither of us had slept very well, so we both rolled out of bed at the crack of dawn. Ed got dressed and went outside to do some chores around the yard and watch the sunrise while I got Lulu's prune juice under way. As I was going through the pantry for breakfast materials, I suddenly felt overcome with the heat and suffocating humidity and unthinkingly opened a kitchen window.

Wham! The deafening burglar alarm system went off, and I knew it also went off at nearby police headquarters. Because the shutoff panel for the system was on the wall in Burnsy's bedroom closet, I raced down the hall to his room, knocked on the door, and pushed it open.

Burnsy was already out of bed and had a fresh cigar smouldering away. He was standing in his droopy boxer shorts in front of his bed, blinking absently, totally ignoring the din of the alarm , and me. I suddenly remembered how deaf he was, and went over to him and pointed to his closet door, screaming "I have to get in there to shut it off! Please open it for me."

He waved his cigar at the closet door, indicating I should go and open it. I yanked open the door, pawed through a bunch of shirts and pants on hangers, and found the shutoff panel. I pulled open the little metal door and banged on the on-off switch, but the deafening noise continued without a pause.

At that moment I heard a siren through the other din, looked out of Burnsy's window, and, sure enough, here came the gendarmes. As I turned to go out to let them in, Lulu, her face a mishmash of some kind of gooey skin cream, roared into the bedroom. waving her arms and yelling over the din, "What the hell's going on in here," she screeched at me. "Who set off that damned alarm? And why are you in my husband's bedroom,"

I demurred, shaking my head in utter confusion.

Suddenly, for reasons unknown, the alarm shut itself off, leaving Lulu still standing there in her nightgown screaming in the sudden silence at me and Burnsy. Then I saw two policemen leering quizzically through the hall door behind Lulu. They had apparently come in through the kitchen door towards the sound of the alarm.

"What's the problem, here, ladies?" one of them asked of no one in particular.

"The alarm went off when I opened a window to get some fresh air, officer," I gasped, "and I couldn't shut it off. I'm really sorry to have you men come up here again. It's all my fault. I apologize profoundly."

Lulu suddenly saw herself in Burnsy's mirror, panicked, and dashed past me in her own bedroom, screeching as she went by me, "I'll deal with you later, you dumb broad."

Burnsy turned to watch her as she scrambled down the hall, shook his head, scratched it, and blew a large cloud of cigar smoke after her. "She's the dumb broad," he muttered.

The two cops discreetly made their departure, one saying to me with a quiet smile, "I've been here before. Looks like you've got yourself quite a zoo here." I couldn't have said it better.

But I never heard anything more about that early morning squall. I guess Lulu was so undone by her mirrored image that she figured she'd better let sleeping dogs lie. Including Lovable.

She even forgot her morning prune juice..

Cops and Hormones at the Gala

Ed reports. . .

We knew by now that our Lululand sojurn was about to come to an end. We hadn't had one day off in nearly a month. Jackie's mother was now in seriously declining health back in Fresno, and we were totally disillusioned by the phony picture of this job painted for us originally by Lulu. But the last climactic episode of our stay was, in retrospect, hysterical.

I had been directed by Lulu to have the limo ready to take them to a gala fund-raising theatrical show to be held in the evening at a local auditorium on the outskirts of the city. Lulu, as a large benefactor of the affair, was to be a featured speaker.

I had already picked them up in at their offices, Jackie had cooked and I had served their dinner earlier than usual, and I now waited until they had dressed for the occasion. Lulu , amazingly, also had given us permission for Jackie to accompany me in the front seat so we could perhaps do some evening shopping after we dropped them off at their benefit show.

The madame finally appeared in a stunning red beaded evening gown, cut way down to there, with Burnsy padding along behind her in a rumpled tux, tie askew, and wisps of earth-toned gray hair sticking out from under a black fedora. His fixture cigar gave off its usual whorls of revolting blue smoke.

As I opened the door for them and moved out to the limo, both Jackie and I complimented them on how great they both looked. We got them aboard, and, sure enough, Lovable, yapping happily, scampered past me and up to the back seat window, her usual perch.

"Everybody ready?" I asked over my shoulder. Lulu nodded, Burnsy puffed a cloud, Lovable yip-yipped, and we were off.

We wound our way down the hills and out into the suburbs to the area where the big event was taking place. On arrival at the mammoth auditorium, we noted several other large limos, some of them bearing state or federal license plates, already parked. Lots of big muckey-mucks, we figured. Should give Lulu great exposure.

I got out, went around to their curbside door, and helped them out.

"Ed, be back here at 11:00. And be prompt, understand?" Lulu rasped. I nodded and watched them melt into the forming crowd at the entrance.

I got back into the limo with Jackie and we slowly rolled back towards town along a route that we hadn't been on before.

"You sure we're headed towards the store?" Jackie asked.

I nodded, saying, "We're on the opposite side of town from what we're used to. But I'm heading in the right direction."

Suddenly we were there at a big mall complex, just where we wanted to be.

I pulled to the side of the road. The limo was just too big to park comfortably anywhere in the mall's lot. I turned on the radio and dozed off while Jackie went into one of the department stores.

Suddenly she was back with several bags of stuff she'd picked up from her shopping safari. "Wake up, Ed. We have to pick them up soon." She got in as Lovable awoke in the back seat and began her usual frantic yapping.

"We may as well wend our way back to the party," Jackie advised. "Better be early than sorry. I can't imagine Lulu waiting on the curb for anyone."

We'd gone about a mile when I suddenly saw flashing lights in my rear view mirror, followed by a quick siren's wail. The police car came alongside, and one of the two officers waved us over to the curb.

I did as I was told. But I hadn't been speeding, that was for sure. I hadn't run any stop signs. What had I done?

"Please, let me see your driver's license and your registration," the cop said, flipping through his record pad. He came around to Jackie's side of the car and watched as she opened the glove compartment and got the registration. I pulled out my wallet for my license as he said,.

" Kind of late to be out in a rig like this, isn't it?" The officer then scanned our papers with his flashlight asking us who we were and why we were out at night in a big stretch limo all by ourselves.

We explained our jobs, who we worked for,and said we were on our way back to pick up our employers at the big benefit show over at that suburban auditorium.

He nodded, then looked around in the open glove compartment, and saw a vial of something among all the papers and other driver's trivia.

"Please let me see that little bottle," he asked. Jackie reached in and handed it to him.

"What's this stuff?" he asked. We both shook our heads and said we had no idea what it was. It surely wasn't ours.

The officer looked over our papers once more, and again his hand with the plastic vial which appeared to contain some little white pills, and went back to his car, reaching into it for his radio mike. I watched him say something to his headquarters, then read off our license number. He came back to my side of the car and I asked him why he had stopped us.

"One of your tail lights is out," he said. "Please follow me to headquarters."

"What for," I hollered at him as he got back into his patrol car and started to drive away. In response, he just waved at me to follow him. We had no choice but to do so.

I looked at my watch. It was nearly eleven o'clock. Lulu and Burnsy would be coming out of the show soon. Jeez.

We rolled into the parking lot of the police precinct office behind the officer who beckoned for us to follow him inside.

He went to a desk officer, apparently telling him about us as he shook the vial of pills back and forth. Another officer came by the desk and picked up the pill bottle and disappeared.

"Officer," I demanded. "Why are we here? We've broken no law. You're holding us illegally. And we've got to be back to pick up Mr. and Mrs. Kandahar at 11:00 over at that auditorium."

"You're going nowhere until we get a report back from our lab as to just what was in that bottle of pills you had in the limo."

Jackie and I looked blankly at each other. She said, "Looks like we're going to have to call Lulu at the show, have her paged, and then have them come over here by taxi so we can explain all this."

"You gotta be kidding," I exclaimed.

"Got any better ideas?" I didn't.

So we got the desk officer, an older man, to place a call to the auditorium requesting a paging call for Mr. and Mrs. Kandahar.

After several minutes, as the officer drummed on his desk with a pencil, he apparently got Lulu on the phone.

"Mrs. Kandahar?" he said in that flat policeman's voice. "Do you have a man and a woman named Hibler driving your Cadillac limousine?"

We could hear Lulu's trombone voice bellowing on the other end, clear across the room.

"Well, come on down here and clear up a few things, please. We will expect you here within the hour. " He hung up and asked us, "Was that *the* Lorraine Kandahar, the gal who used to run with the wolves around here in the old days?"

We nodded. "That's her."

"Well, we're sorry for all this inconvenience, but we need to know just what kind of stuff you—or she—have been hauling around in that limo. Once that's cleared up you can probably go home."

Within twenty minutes a battered yellow cab pulled up in front of headquarters and Lulu stumbled out, followed by Burnsy, his black fedora jammed down over his ears, struggling along behind her. Lovable, still in the back of the limo, began yapping as she saw her beloved mistress stomping by.

Lulu slammed open the swinging doors of the office and headed for the desk sergeant.

"Where are those two?" she roared. "I want to kill 'em. They ruined my whole goddam evening. What have they done?" She banged her beaded purse on the desk sergeant's head. Two other officers came in from an adjoining room and restrained her. We were on the opposite side of the room from where she had come in and I called over to her, "We're over here, Mrs. Kandahar, and we haven't done a thing. . ."

She grabbed her purse off the officer's desk—he was still rubbing his head—and came over to me, eyes blazing.

"You two nitwits are fired.," she sizzled. "I want you out of my place by the end of the week."

Just then, the officer who had taken that vial of pills from the arresting officer, came in with them in his hand and gave them to the desk officer.

"These are a prescription for hormones—estrogen," he said.

The desk officer blushed deeply and handed them to Lulu, who by now was seething with rage.

"Of all the outrages," she ranted. "What in hell were you doing with my prescription?" She swung her purse again at that same desk officer she'd belted before, but this time he ducked. He shoved his chair away from the desk, stood up and roared, "Get the hell out of here, all of you!" He strode to the door, opened it and pointed out at the limo. "And get that damned tail light fixed."

We did get the hell out of there, and not a word passed between any of us on the way back to the palace. Even Lovable kept her mouth shut.

We delivered them to the house, I put the limo in the garage, buttoned up the alarm system and slunk off to bed. Neither Jackie nor I had said a word to each other all the way home. Now, as we squirmed down into bed, Jackie said, "Well, looks like we have another chapter for that book coming up."

Thoroughly depressed, I murmured an uh-huh, and fell asleep.

Well, we had now been fired before we had had a chance to quit. But we were both actually relieved, especially after all the increasing verbal abuse from this crazy woman, which was becoming worse by the day.

She had been avoiding us ever since our wild evening, but now, on that next week-end, I had to tell her we were about to leave, and I asked her for our last pay check. Apparently she had already made it out, and yanked it out of her purse, snapping, "Good riddance."

By now we had retrieved our repaired gimpy motor home from our out-of-town friends. Ed brought it up to the back of the house to load up our stuff. Within two hours we had everything we'd brought with us packed and in either the motor home or the little Datsun. Lulu and Burnsy were visiting somewhere so we had no fond farewells.

But just before we backed out of the driveway en route for a couple of days off—finally—with the same friends who had helped us out before, I suddenly had an overwhelming desire to raise one last bit of hell with Lulu. The kitchen door was still unlocked before I made a last security check. I quickly went in and tripped the burglar alarm.

I backed out the motor home, Jackie followed closely in the Datsun. We listened to that alarm din as we drove slowly down the street. We stopped at the next corner and waited. I wanted to watch the cops and fire engines roar in once more.

They roared in, we cheered quietly to ourselves, I gave Jackie a high-five in the mirror, then we rolled out of Lululand.

CHAPTER 4

Meanwhile,
Back At the Ranch With Sin-Bed

Ed reports. . .

Several days before leaving Lulu's kooky nest, we had seen two new ads in local papers, and another came from Joan, all asking for a couple to manage estate property in the North Bay area. Hers sounded more interesting. The day before we left looney Lulu and Burnsy, we called the advertising party for an appointment for the following Monday.

The plush place was located on a hillside in the Alexander Valley, another wine-growing area well north of Napa and St.Helena. Interviewing us was a middle-aged, slightly-built, darkly handsome man, swarthy and mustachioed, seemingly of Middle-Eastern or Southern European ethnic origin. He introduced himself as Ahmed Disrahlbi, and described himself as a commercial real estate and manufacturing entrepreneur with international connections. He was dressed in an immaculate white linen suit with ascot tie and white casual shoes.

We met in his spacious ranch house living room, noting that he appeared brusque in manner, and seemed to relish using an unblinking steely gaze to face down others. Noting that I was a retired professor, he revealed that he was himself American university-educated. He spoke flawless English with a barely discernible accent.

We found, as time passed, that he was clearly used to dominating any group. We also noted later that he immensely enjoyed playing the gracious host at elegant house and lawn parties thrown periodically for the international set of the Bay Area. He called ambassadors and other pajandrums of the international business set, by their first names, and loved to charm the ladies with his continental hand-kissing manners He also apparently has had mysterious connections with many politically powerful figures in other countries where he had large business property holdings. We later became aware that many phone calls came to this ranch house, often in the wee hours of the night, indicating that they probably originated half-way around the world.

We also discovered that there had been two unsuccessful apparent attempts on his life, both drive-by shootings, apparently by either overseas business competitors or thugs with political connections to his enemies. One long-range shot went through his bedroom window. Rumor had it that guns hired by Middle-Eastern operatives were out to get him.

Our most chilling later discovery was that a year or so earlier one of his ranch workers had been found shot dead, his body found hanging from a large oak tree on the ranch, an enigmatic warning note pinned to his clothing.

We soon were to dub him, between ourselves, Sin-Bed, with the hyphen deliberate. Sin-Bed, we soon discovered, was usually only on the property during week-ends. Ah, but those week-ends.

He showed us our prospective quarters near the carport area, then gave us a long orientation drive around his really magnificent hilly, 500-acre oak-studded estate, showing us what we individually would be responsible for. After a quick exchange of glances and discreet nods with Jackie at the end of our little tour, we agreed to take the job, although at slightly less money than at vulturesville. At least it was an escape from the lunacy of Lululand.

Thus, after a week or so of unwinding and visiting our benevolent friends who had saved our motor home earlier that year, and briefly checking on our still threatened home some 200 miles away, we went to work for Sin-Bed.

Our new digs were in a tiny one-bedroom cottage adjacent to the big ranch house; our duties were the usual for a caretaker-manager couple. But this time Jackie had no cooking to do, just care of the big sprawling house, and help with the large lawn and house parties Sin-Bed liked to throw periodically.

The sprawling one-story house itself was comfortably furnished with leather ranch-style sofas and lounge chairs. Floors were of heavy Spanish-style bronze tile. Prints of hunting scenes and other landscapes, some of them clearly from Middle Eastern countries, hung on wood-planking walls. A massive fieldstone fireplace dominated one wall of the living room. Two wings of tastefully furnished bedrooms with adjoining baths extended from both side of the main house, virtually surrounding a large swimming pool.

My work was to maintain four tennis courts, keep the spacious lawns mowed and trimmed, service the large pool, prune fruit trees, seasonally replant and fertilize flowers, bulbs, and shrubs as needed around the place, and make sure that guests, especially female, were properly esconced in their very comfortable quarters near the pool. Jackie had a full-time job just maintaining the huge house, though, thankfully, as noted, she had no cooking chores

Our first week or so with Sin-Bed seemed to go fairly smoothly. Both Jackie and I had a lot of new routines to learn and adjust to. But because Sin-Bed spent the bulk of most week-days at his office in The City, and was on the ranch usually only on week-ends, we had a fairly relaxing period to get adjusted.

I spent much of this period roaming around the sprawling ranch and learning where water connections and other utilities were located. Because the bulk of the entire ranch was on a mountain side, it meant a lot of hard climbing any time I needed to explore. Usually to accompany me on my walks when Jackie was busy in the house, would be Butch, Sin-Bed's affable border collie. Also in residence were a couple of feral cats who spent much of their time on the roof, out of range of Butch.

One of the first things I noted about the place was that it had virtually no machinery or other labor-saving equipment for maintenance. It especially needed a pickup truck, and on the first weekend Sin-Bed visited after our arrival, I told him that the place badly needed one. He listened as I told him how much help it would be and how it would speed up many of the maintenance chores around the place as well as improve security. He liked that security idea, and finally agreed. Because he said he knew nothing about buying a truck, asked me to go with him into town and get one the next day, a Saturday.

We picked up a nicely maintained used small four-wheel-drive import pickup, equipped with a CB radio, for which Sin-Bed wrote out a check on the spot. He wanted to try it out on the way home, but discovered it had a stick shift which he had never learned to use. So I took over the driving while he drove his Mercedes back to the ranch. However, he asked me to follow him first to a large sporting goods store where he apparently spent both a lot of time and money.

We walked into the place and he went directly to the gun department and asked to see new models of deer rifles. He called me over with him to ask my opinion.

"I really know little about guns, sir," I said, "though I have used .22s when I was a kid and later with my sons and grandchildren. And I have done some team pistol shooting. But why do you want a rifle?"

"You will need it in the new pickup," he said, giving me a strange smile, "and you will also need a gun rack to go with it."

We walked over to a display of truck gun racks. He picked one out, and then moved over to a display rack of rifles. He tossed me a .30-.30 carbine to heft. I sighted it around the room and told him it had a good balance.

"Good," he said. "Let's get some ammunition and get on home. I want you to get some practice using it." I gulped.

We left the store and headed back to the ranch, he in the Mercedes, me in the new pickup, with the new gun rack, ammo and rifle stacked on the seat beside me.

I looked at the rifle with a strange feeling of uneasiness, for I knew this guy was no hunter, and wondered just what he had in mind. I soon found out.

I drove the new truck into an empty space in the large carport, and got out just as Sin-Bed drove in behind me. He put the Mercedes away and beckoned for me to follow him into his home office at the rear of the ranch house.

His office was paneled in walnut, with scenes from around the world framed on the walls. A number of testimonials and plaques, some of them apparently in Arabic, were also evident. He asked me to sit down across from his desk.

"Ed," he said in his customary brusque manner, "as you know, I'm away from this place most of each week. And I have had several incidents here involving gunshots in the past few months, which disturb me, I don 't want to get our local police involved for personal reasons.

"But I will need you to make regular tours around this property, and on an irregular time schedule, as a security patrol. I know I didn't mention this during our first interview, but at that time it didn't seem to be that important. Within the past several weeks it has become so. That is why I felt you needed a long-range rifle with you in the truck on your patrols, just in case."

He got up from his desk, walked over to a window overlooking the broad valley below, now darkening in the early dusk. Lights from the nearby city were beginning to wink on. He turned and gave me another of his patented steely stares and said, "And there's another thing you and Jackie should be aware of."

"Oh?" I queried. "And what might that be?"

"Well, Ed, I have a very dear lady friend who visits me out here ocasionally, and I want you both to meet her and become acquainted. You will find this lady friendly and helpful at times when I may not be around or available. Her name is Miss Longstreet.

"Because she is here so frequently, I have maintained a special wing of the house for her exclusive use, and I want you to tell

Jackie to pay special attention to that part of the house and keep it neat and immaculate at all times." He paused and gave me an especially direct stare. "It is critical that there be nothing left in her quarters after she leaves which might be found by others. No hairpins, curlers, or you know, women's things. Understand?"

I nodded as I began to see what kind of a relationship he had going here. I then asked, "Mr. Disrahlbi, would you mind telling me just what or who it is that you feel threatened by, and why you think you need an armed guard patrolling this place. I really. . ."

He interrupted me abruptly, saying, "Yes, I do mind. All you need to know is to keep a sharp eye out for trespassers and use your CB radio in the truck to call the house home station. Do not ever call the police. I don't want them fooling around my property. I have no respect for them whatever.

"That's all, Ed. I'll see you in the morning. And, thank you for your help in picking out the truck I hope it meets your needs. Do you have anything else you or Jackie need in your cottage?"

Amazing, I thought. Here was a man who actually was concerned about his help, despite his apparent brusqueness.

I said that we could use a couple of comfortable reclining chairs in our living room to replace the badly worn day bed that was currently there, but that otherwise we were in good shape. I told him we would do our best to be of help to him around his ranch.

He was sitting down to make phone calls as I left his office, telling me to go into town the next day and get whatever we needed for our apartment. He handed me a credit card to use for any purchases.

My mind raced. Just what did he fear? And how come he was getting us involved in what should be a police matter? And why didn't he trust the police?

I told Jackie at bedtime of our day with the new pickup, the rifle and gun rack, and his strange behavior.

"What's he afraid of? How come he's asking you to maybe be a target?" she asked.

I shrugged. and said, "Let's not borrow trouble. He at least has told us to go into town tomorrow and get us a couple of decent recliners for the living room."

Neither of us slept very well that night.

Autumn mornings around the ranch were usually spectacular, with bright sunshine shimmering through huge pines pand glowing golden leaves on surrounding massive oaks. There often was morning valley fog which gave the whole area below the house the look of a great sea, with hill tops peeking above the overcast like islands before the later sun burned it all away.

On one particular morning, a few days after my office talk with Sin-Bed, I decided to try out the new truck with its four-wheel drive option. I had already installed the gun rack and rifle at the rear of the cab, and called old Butch to come for a ride. He leaped in and immediately stuck his head out the window for some windy fresh air.

We slowly made our way around the many unpaved side tracks on the property as I studied the whole area for the first time with Sin-Bed's warning stuck in my mind. It was a gorgeously clear sunny day, with a light breeze blowing, making golden waves in the undulating grasses on the hills. In the far distance, barely visible, were several hot air balloons from the lower Sonoma valley floating lazily like colored gum drops. It was peace personified.

Clang! A heavy thud from something hitting the side of the truck was accompanied simultaneously with the stinging crack of a rifle shot. Butch bellowed and leaped out of the window, disappearing. I froze momentarily, then threw the stick into four-wheel drive and careened around a shoulder of a nearby rise, just missing Butch by inches. I stopped, got out the passenger's door and crawled gingerly behind the tailgate while trying to find out who had been shooting at us, if indeed we were a target. Even though I had Sin-Bed's new .30-.30 carbine with me, I wasn't about to get into any kind of a gun fight with anyone.

Then around the end of another rise of a nearby hill, came a full-size battered pickup with two whooping and hollering redneck types, roaring all over the landscape, firing rifles in the air, laughing and hooting all the way.

Suddenly they noticed my truck with me peering over the tailgate, and stopped abruptly. "Hey, you wanna beer? " one of the two bellowed at me. I shook my head and they threw their truck into gear and turned towards me. I felt cold running through my gut as they got closer.

But neither of them seemed belligerent; they seemed to be just two drunks out on a toot. When they got up to me, the one who offered me the beer tossed a bottle at me anyway and burbled, "Live it up a little. 'S hot today. He tossed his head back and emptied his own bottle and reached down to open another.

I finally got enough wits together to walk over to them. They had a big cross-breed pit bull in the bed of the truck who growled and bellowed menacingly as I came up to their truck. "Hannibal, shuddup and get down," roared one of them at the menacing dog.

I cleared a dry throat and said with as much authority as I could muster,

"Hey, do you guys know you hit my truck with a rifle shot, and that you 're trespassing on private property? And that discharging a firearm in this county is a felony?"

The two of them, both clearly drunk as frogs, looked at each other, tossed their heads back and roared with laughter. "We're tres-*pissin'* he says," the driver said, smirking at me. "We ain't been pissin' anywhere, but I think's a good idea. You been pissin' any, Jake?" Jake blinked blurry eyes and shook his tousled head.

"Well, buddy," the driver sneered at me, "We ain't hurting no one, an' Thanksgivin' s comin' soon an' we're just celebratin' a little early. Thought we might even get us a wild turkey out here. Sure you don't want a good cold beer?" He held another bottle up.

I shook my head again and tried a little diplomacy. Clearing my throat, I said "Tell you what," I said, "If you guys will turn around and leave this property without any more gunfire, I won't call in the police on my radio. Now be good guys and go sleep it off."

They looked groggily at each other again, one of them spit a stream of tobacco juice out his window, then the driver shrugged and threw his truck into gear and roared off with Hannibal bellowing all the way. They bounced wildly across the open slope back towards a secondary gate usually kept locked on the far side of the property. I took down their license number and followed them in our truck until I was sure they were leaving, and checked the gate they had forced open. The chain connecting two padlocks on the gatepost had been cut twice with bolt cutters.

I checked the back of our truck and found a bullet hole just above the filler cap of the gas tank. God, I thought. It was only a foot from the gas tank itself.

"They could have blown us away," I said to Butch as he jumped back into the cab. I decided that Sin-Bed had better be told of my encounter. Perhaps those two characters were more than just a couple of drunks trespassing.

Back at the house I called him at his office in the City and reported the incident.

"You didn't call the police, did you?" he snapped.

I demurred, and he calmed down, saying "Well, you apparently handled it right, Ed. Probably only a couple of dumb drunks out on a binge."

Yeah, I thought, as I hung up. Probably.

Loving Elegance Arrives

Jackie reports. . .

By the end of the second week with Sin-Bed, we were pretty well settled into our new routine. Then one morning he called me into his office.

He was sitting behind his enormous hand-carved desk. "Good morning, Jackie," he smiled through heavy horn-rimmed glasses, displaying those perfectly aligned, dazzling white teeth. "How are things going for you two now?"

"Just fine," I replied, not quite knowing what he was getting at.

"Good. But I wanted to tell you that my friend, Miss Longstreet, will be coming out to the ranch later today and will stay several days with us. I want you and Ed to meet her and become acquainted. You may need to work with her at times when I'm away. I'm sure you will like her.

"Miss Longstreet is office manager and vice president of a large international exporting firm in the City, but when she visits out here at the ranch on week-ends she helps me with some of my overseas contacts. It's easier for her to come out here than for me to go into her office in town during the week."

I nodded, smiled and thought, "I'll just bet it's easier for her to come out here." But I said, "I'm sure we will get along just fine, Mr. Disrahlbi. We will do our best to make her feel comfortable. Is there anything else you need?"

He at first shook his head, then swiveled around to his fax machine, saying, "Yes, one more thing. Please be absolutely certain that her bathroom and bedroom are entirely free of any items like hair pins, curlers, and so on. Mrs. D will be visiting here soon. But just be sure that Miss Longstreet is comfortable. I will be away today during the afternoon when she arrives, but will be through my work in time to meet her in town for dinner."

I left his office wondering just what kind of a woman we were going to be meeting. Somehow I visualized a brassy, busty bimbo type, probably chewing gum and wearing tight Spandex pants and stiletto heels. But that mental pictured didn't fit the office manager-vice president image. I just didn't know what to expect. I also wondered if this relationship was known to Mrs. Disrahlbi, a woman we had not yet met. That afternoon brought a stunning surprise.

The ranch house, like Lulu's palace, was fitted with all kinds of sophisticated burglar alarms and warning bells, and immediately after our arrival, Sin-Bed had showed us what he called the annunciator system of bells which rang both in his house office and in our quarters as well. Thus whenever anyone turned in to the ranch entry road from the main highway at the gate in the valley below, the car's wheels would run over a switch which rang the bells at the ranch some half-mile above the entrance. Sin-Bed also kept a pair of powerful tripod-mounted binoculars trained on the locked entrance gate, as well as on the telephone installed by the gate for visitor communication. Thus with the powerful glasses we could tell immediately who was coming up to the house, and even read the license plates on arriving cars.

Late that afternoon after he had left, we heard the double bong-bong from the annunciator and knew someone was on the way up. I ran into the boss's office to the binoculars and saw what looked like a new red Mercedes convertible edging its way through the gate, though I couldn't make out who was driving. It usually took about five to six minutes for a car to drive from the gate to the house, so I scrambled around to make doubly sure that Miss Longstreet's quarters were ready for her, if indeed this was who was coming up the hill.

It was.

Her sleek convertible turned into the carport area, stopped, and as Ed joined me, we watched a truly elegant lady emerge. This was no bimbo, I thought, as she approached us with hand outstretched and a dazzling smile.

"You must be Jackie and Ed," she said, shaking hands with us both. "I'm Ada. Ahmed has been telling me marvelous things about you both."

Ed went to her car and retrieved a suitcase and small makeup kit. Somehow this whole meeting momentarily seemed out of synch. The lady just didn't fit the stereotype of a "mistress," but that's clearly what she was. Strangely, I immediately felt a warm bond with this woman, perhaps because I had been cut off for so long from seeing so many of my own women friends now hundreds of miles away. She seemed so filled with bubbling happy enthusiasm. I immediately liked her, as did Ed.

As he went with her to take her luggage to her quarters, I had a chance to really size up an extraordinary woman. She was, I guessed, in her early fifties, tall, very pretty, slender, with a lovely figure, and immaculately dressed in what seemed to be designer sports clothes well chosen for a casual week-end in the country. Smiling cornflower blue eyes dramatically contrasted with her strawberry blonde hair which she wore in a beautifully coiffed and sculptured halo. Ada had the smooth, lightly tanned skin of a twenty-year-old, and moved with the grace of a totally poised dancer. She was a woman who clearly had taken good care of herself and had been able to afford the best in body care treatments.

We later discovered that she had been divorced for many years, had three grown sons and two daughters, and was not only a graduate of the University of California, but also had earned a MBA degree. Hardly a bimbo.

I went into our tiny kitchen to get us dinner while we watched the evening news on our new little television. In a half hour or so, Ada poked her head into our small living room, saying, "Have a great evening. I'm going into town to meet Ahmed for dinner. I'm sure happy you two are here. I'm really looking forward to getting better acquainted." She waved as she backed the convertible out of the carport and drove down the hill.

A classy lady, we both agreed. But we wondered how someone with such panache could live as a kept woman. Or was she, really? We would learn much more very soon.

That Sinister Call

Ed reports. . .

My work fell into a daily routine that became easier to manage as time passed. I'd usually get up about six a. m., have a quick bite with Jackie, then go out to sweep the pool, feed Butch and the two half-wild cats who hung around the place, then either mow the large lawn, prune trees, gather cut flowers for the house, or dead-head others, or begin replantings, depending upon the season.

About once every two weeks I'd pressure-hose and swab down the four tennis courts.

One apparently routine Friday morning was interrupted with an enigmatic phone call. Some man with a basso-profundo voice and thick accent was asking for Sin-Bed who was in the City at his office on this particular morning. I told the caller that he wasn't available but that he could probably be reached in the City. The caller, clearly in an ugly mood, snarled that he'd already called him there and that he wasn't there. In that thick accent he warned,

"Tell that sonabitch he better be at meeting tomorrow, or he lose a lot more than money. Tell him Kamar called." I asked him to please spell his name. "K-a-m-a-r," he snapped, then the phone banged down, hard.

I wrote a quick note to Sin-Bed about the call and left it on his office desk.

Kamar? Sounded Arabic to me. The call left me very uneasy, especially after the rumors we'd heard about his problems with overseas countries where it was said that he had lost confiscated property. He'd already had two drive-by long-range shootings, one of which shattered his bedroom window. But he had refused to call in police. I told Jackie about the call, but she felt that it was none of our business, and that we shouldn't get involved with Sin-Bed's personal problems.

"Hell, we're already involved, whether we like it or not," I shot back. "I've already had two supposed drunks put a rifle shot through my truck—and it could have been my head— and during the past several days I've noticed with the binocs several cars slowing way down right by our gate, big cars, and filled with men. They were still too far away to get any idea of who they were, but this whole business is beginning to give me the willies."

We were interrupted by the annunciator's bong-bong, and figured that would be Sin-Bed arriving for another the week-end with Ada. In scarcely three minutes—Sin-Bed was a wild driver— he screeched up the winding road into the carport area and stepped out. He greeted us with his usual polite but enigmatic "Hello," and immediately strode quickly into his office.

I could tell that he was preoccupied with something, but I called Ada in her room to let her know that he had arrived, and went about my routine. Within minutes he called me into his office, looking deadly pale.

"Tell me about this phone call," he said, holding up my note with a trembling hand.

"Nothing more to say, sir, except that the caller appeared to be very angry. He said you'd know who he was, and said you'd better be at some kind of a meeting tomorrow—or else, as he put it. I. . ."

He interrupted me with an abrupt dismissal wave of a hand, saying "You are not to mention this to anyone; not Miss Longstreet, not anyone. Understand?" I nodded and left.

Later he and beautiful Ada left in her convertible for another in-town dinner, saying they'd be back before midnight.

At about eleven o'clock that evening we heard a distant metallic crashing sound, like an automobile crash, but in the dark I couldn't use the binocs to check on where it was coming from. But immediately we could hear the sound of a powerful motor roaring up the grade towards us. Someone had crashed the gate and was coming hell-bent for the house. I asked Jackie to turn out all the lights in our place and get down out of sight. "Damn," I muttered, "why did we take Butch to the vet yesterday? We could sure use him now. This looks like trouble.".

It was.

A large dark-colored van roared into the parking area behind the carport and screeched to a stop. We were peering in the dark from behind our curtains to see if we could make out who it was. But with the outside lights out there was little to see except for three or four dark shapes moving quickly through the carport gate down towards the house. We could hear brief low-voiced exchanges between them, but couldn't make out what was being said.

I then realized I had left the sliding doors to the house by the pool unlocked after Sin-Bed left. They immediately found the opening. We could hear thudding, a couple of crashes, then a lot of banging, cursing and yelling from what seemed to be Sin-Bed's office. Jackie mentioned to me later that at that moment she had thought about the dull routine life we had left at home—and now look where we were. At the same moment I had thought to myself, how in hell did we ever get into these things? First Jackie's leg disaster, then Lulu's nightmare. Now this. Ye gods!

At this moment the phone rang and someone in the house immediately picked it up. I dared to very gingerly pick up our extension and heard a gutteral voice growling, "The bastard's not here," and then something unintelligible in a foreign language; again, it sounded like Arabic. I very softly hung up the phone.

Jackie and I were terrified but dared not make a sound. In another five minutes or so the bunch of intruders came back through the open carport gate, pausing briefly to bang on our door. Then, when they heard nothing from inside, they continued out to their van and took off.

We went immediately into the house to see what they had done to the place, and found his office a shambles. His desk lamp was smashed on the floor with pencils and other debris scattered around. File drawers were open with papers tossed everywhere. His leather recliner had a long vicious slash in it clear from the top of the back down through the seat. Several of his wall plaques and pictures had been thrown against the wall and smashed. We noticed some sort of a note in the middle of the desk written in what looked like Arabic with a large felt pen , but couldn't read it.

We dared not call the police because of Sin-Bed's warnings, so we just left things the way we found them and waited for his return.

He and Ada arrived back from their dinner date shortly after midnight, scarcely half an hour after our invasion. We met them in the carport as they drove in, and immediately told what had happened, and that they had missed meeting the intruders by less than half an hour.

Both of them blanched at our story ."We wondered what had happened to the gate as we came in," Ada said as they quickly hurried into the house and surveyed the damage, while we stayed discreetly in our own place. Sin-Bed immediately called us from his office on the intercom. "Please come in here, both of you," he requested.

Both he and Ada were sorting through the mess as we reached his office.

I said, "At your request we didn't call the police, but we were terrified. We had all our lights out and stayed hidden in our place till they left."

Sin-Bed, his hands trembling, said, "I'm glad you weren't hurt. But please tell me what you heard. Did you hear anything they said, or what they wanted?"

I told him about my sneaking a listen on our phone extension, but that they appeared to be speaking a foreign language that could have been Arabic."

"Arabic? How would you know anything about Arabic?" Sin-Bed asked.

"We've traveled extensively in the Middle East and heard enough of it to recognize the inflections and some of the words."

"Oh? Well, you understand you are to say absolutely nothing about this to anyone, understand? " We both nodded. "I will take care of this matter in my own way." He turned abruptly from us and put his arms around Ada who suddenly had burst into tears.

"I'm afraid, Ahmed," she sobbed. "For you—and for all of us here."

Sin-Bed said over his shoulder to us, abruptly , "Goodnight."
It was anything but.

The Plot Thickens

Jackie reports. . .

The next morning Sin-Bed was up even before our usual early rising, and left well before six o'clock without saying where he was going or when he might be back. He no doubt was headed for that meeting he'd been warned about, wherever that was. Ada remained at the house.

Later on in the morning she appeared in the living room where I was cleaning, and asked me to sit with her for a few minutes. I put down my dusting cloths and sat down beside her on one of the leather couches.

"Jackie," she began, "I'm terribly sorry you and Ed have become involved with this problem of Ahmed's. I don 't really know what to do to help except perhaps help you find another place to work. But you have both been so helpful to both him and me we don't want to lose you."

She paused and then asked me, "I've wondered, just how in the world did two people like you, both university educated, and you, Ed, with a doctorate, and at your ages, wind up doing house and landscape work, especially here?"

I smiled and told her the whole sad story of our financial debacle, our attempts to recoup some of the loss by managing a retirement home, my leg accident and the turmoil that followed it, our weird experiences with Lulu and company, and of our friends Bob and Joan who had had similar experiences in their own lives.

Ada listened with tears welling up in those beautiful cornflower blue eyes.

"You two are really amazing people. I'm so glad you came here to be with us. I told Ahmed I thought he had picked a couple of gems when he got you two. But now with this sudden violence here I'm torn betwen wanting you to get away and wanting you to stay. I know we can become very good friends."

I felt for a moment that she probably needed friends, and after feeling so isolated myself, I knew I could use a good friend and confidant. I know Sin-Bed expected us to always address Ada as "Miss Longstreet," and to be helpful and polite. And from things he had said about his experiences with former employees, he neither encouraged or approved of such friendships. Yet I felt that a strong bond was growing with Ada, and I couldn't ignore those feelings. Then her next suggestion made it even more difficult to simply play the "servant" role. I now knew that Ed and I needed her as much as she needed us.

She dabbed at her eyes, looked at her watch, and said. "It's almost noon. Tell you what. Go get Ed and and tell him to get changed and I'll take you both to lunch. It'll do us all good to get out of here for a while. How about it?"

I was stunned at the invitation, but replied that Ahmed might not like to have his lady friend consorting with the help.

"Nonsense!" she said. "I invite whom I wish to entertain when I wish. If he doesn't like it, that's his problem." She suddenly gave me a hug and said, "Now go get dressed and call Ed. We're heading for lunch."

But before I could call Ed she was back from her room carrying a tiny bottle of perfume which she handed to me. I looked at the label. It read "*Poison.*"

Ada said, "Please take this, Jackie. It's my favorite. Ahmed likes it too and is very familiar with the scent. I uncorked the little bottle, sniffed gently, and said, "What a lovely gift, Ada. Amazingly, this is the same perfume Ed gave me before we had our financial disaster. It's my favorite, too."

Ada said quickly, "It's much more than just a token of my feelings for you both. This way if Maria ever notices it in the house after I've left, you can tell her that it is yours." Our growing bond seemed already much closer.

I called Ed in from the garden near the pool where he'd been planting bulbs for a later spring display, and told him about our invitation.

"Do you think we should do this? He might fire us. I don't think . . ."

I interrupted him with, "Look, we've been anchored here now for three weeks; we've been shot at, had the house invaded, and had the devil scared out of us. I'm ready for an escape. Ada's offered to take us to lunch and I want to go.

Ed shrugged, "Okay," he said, and went into the cottage, took off his jeans, changed his shirt, and put on loafers, a sports coat and slacks.

I took a quick shower. And as I looked in the mirror while putting on fresh make-up was it my imagination, or were those lines around my eyes and mouth always that deep? Well, I thought, nothing I can do about it but sponge on more make-up and smile a lot. I tried to convince myself, as I sponged and patted, that It made the deeper wrinkles less prominent.

Suddenly I thought of a verse a dear and sensitive friend had written to us recently:

> *Are we really us? And what of us is real?*
> *Two separate selves autonomous,*
> *To harbor all our zeal. Confusion reigns at every turn.*
> *But we are us- -We've made a deal.*

Yes, we had made a deal, but where was it leading us? I felt a chill as I slipped into a pants suit, one of the few "dress-up" clothes I had brought. I glanced at the mirror and felt that at least momentarily I had my own identity back. I hadn't realized how much of myself I had buried and left behind. It had been easier to play a role that way.

I climbed into the back seat of Ada's red Mercedes, noting that the seats were warm from the luxury car's electrical warming system. Ah, this was the life I was meant to live, I murmured to myself. Then Ed got in front with Ada, and off we went.

"Where are you taking us?" I asked Ada.

"To one of the best bistro's in this whole wine-growing area. I know you'll love it. I adore their food—and the view from the dining terrace is tremendous."

After a drive of about half an hour we noticed that we had driven south quite a distance from the Alexander Valley hills, deep into the Napa area, noted for both its wines and its restaurants.

"Here we are," Ada suddenly exclaimed as we drove up a short incline into the parking area of internationally famed Auberge Soleil.

An attendant parked the car as we walked through an exquisite entryway into the dining room and outside terrace which overlooked a huge expanse of the vineyards and winery buildings below. Ed and I both remarked how different these vineyards were from the ones near home in the San Joaquin Valley where the leaves all turn the same color, a dull burnished orange then brown. Here there were purple, red, yellow and beautiful copper tones. At the ends of some of the vineyard rows some of the last red roses of summer still bloomed..

It was another beautiful California fall day with warm sun and light breezes sweeping across those autumn colors of the vineyards, so we chose a table on the terrace for a spectacular view. Ada was right, it was indeed tremendous.

She asked if we would like her to order something special for us. We of course agreed and she gave our order to the attentive waiter, including a fine white wine to go with our lunch.

She leaned forward across the table, looking at us both alternatively, and said, "You must have wondered about my relationship with Ahmed. It's a long story," she said.

"Yes, we had wondered " Ed said. "But you really don't have to get into any of your personal life, you know. Under our present circumstances perhaps we should not know things that are strictly your business." He added, "Considering what has happened over the past several days, the invasion of the house, my being shot at, those phone calls—it all makes us very uneasy. Perhaps the less we know the better off we will be."

I nudged Ed hard under the table. I hoped he would get the point that we should find out everything possible because, like it or not, we were already involved in this mysterious and frightening situation. Ada looked at us, almost pleading.

"I understand that you're a licensed family therapist, Ed," she said, looking directly across the table at him. "and that you, Jackie, have worked with him in his practice. I really need to tell about all this to someone who has no personal involvement. I'd really appreciate it if you could be my confidantes, my therapists. I'll be happy to pay whatever fee you normally charge."

Ed and I exchanged glances. Therapy? From us? Sub-rosa therapists to the girl- friend of our gang-threatened boss? We, who had been shot at and terrified by people who could be international terrorists?

I looked at Ed and he back at me, and said, "We'll be happy to listen, Ada, and, of course, at no charge. You've been very good to us since we came to the ranch and we'd be delighted to help." Ed nodded his agreement.

Ada then proceeded to tell us a fascinating story. She had met Ahmed more than six years earlier at one of his big so-called lawn parties where important people of the international trade set of the Bay area were invited to share a resplendent catered feast of fresh shrimp, rack of lamb, caviar, barbecued filet mignon, champagne and other gourmet delights. Because she was VP and manager of a San Francisco exporting company that sometimes did business with Ahmed, she was on his list of guests.

Apparently, from Ada's story, he was immediately stunned with her, and from that time on proceeded to pursue her relentlessly with flowers, trips to the theater and all the best restaurants and bistros in the area. Eventually, she said, he invited her to accompany him on one of his overseas visits to some of his foreign investments. She went with him and, she said, had the ultimate time of her life. Having spent the last fifteen years being tied to her well-paying job, and dating an occasional dolt from her business contacts, she said she was ready for a dramatic change. Not only that, she found that he was a considerate lover and usually a gallant companion on the golf course and tennis courts, as well as at all of the best watering holes of the North Bay area. She simply fell in love with him.

We listened, enthralled with her story. Then I dared to ask her the ultimate question. "We understand that he has a wife who rarely comes out to the ranch. Is she aware of his relationship with you?"

Ada looked away for a moment, then said, "I really don't know. I have never met her, and Ahmed does his best to make sure that we never meet. But I'm sure she is aware that he has other interests than just his business contacts. After all, he is European, and European men as a group are not noted for their marital fidelity."

She paused a moment, then said, "I know my relationship with this man is not what most people would approve of, but I love him, and I feel sure he feels the same way towards me. He has certainly showered attention on me for the past five years including cars and money and jewelry, clothes and trips to fascinating places."

"Ada," I dared to ask, "Does he also see other women?"

She looked back at me with what clearly was chagrin. "Oh, yes, I'm sure when he is out of town or on a trip that he sees other women friends. But that's his life style. He always comes back to me. The only problem we have had over these years is his intense jealousy and need to totally control me."

"And Maria, his wife, never has been in touch with you?" I asked.

"No, never. And I don't expect that she will be. They apparently have a typical European family relationship. She's the good wife, the mother of his four grown boys, three of whom still live at home with her in the City. The other boy, the youngest, is in school in Switzerland."

Here she paused with what I felt was a wry smile and a bitter comment, "And I am the 'other woman.' I understand that she has become quite obese in her middle years, and that there is very little of an intimate relationship left between them."

She paused in her story as the waiter brought our lunch and wine. It was a spectacular culinary presentation of fine sole with herbs, freshly picked and sauteed vegetables, crusty bread still warm from the oven, and a delightful Chardonnay.

We soon were relaxed over our coffee and a dessert of a delicious light lime sorbet with mint garnish. We now felt more at ease with one another. Ed asked Ada how she was handling Sin-Bed's need, as she had put it, to control her..

"Well, at times it really has been so confining and upsetting that we have temporarily broken up. He has sometimes become violent with me, though he's never actually struck me. It's usually over a lunch meeting or some other contact with men in my business that he objects to. He also wants me to quit my job and spend full time at the ranch, but I have refused. It's still an issue between us.

"In fact I once discovered that he had had my phone tapped for a while. After that happened, I secretly set up my own phone tape recording machine to record anything he said to me on the phone, just in case."

I looked at her intently and said, "Seems to me, Ada, that this affair also includes a lot of distrust. That doesn't bode well for any long term relationship, would you say?"

"I've realized that, but we have had so many good times over these years that I can't imagine living with anyone else or having any other relationship. He's basically a decent man. Jealousy just seems to be a trade mark of European men. They want to not just love you, but own you. But I can't handle that total control bit. It's really been about the only thing we fight over. I keep reminding him that I'm not his wife." Her voice trailed off momentarily as she fought back tears.

I asked her, "Would he divorce his wife and marry you?"

She shook her head and wiped an eye. "No, he won't. He has too much invested in his family to ever give that up, and I've accepted that as part of my relationship with him."

With that she took the bill from the waiter, gave him a credit card, signed it, and we left the table to walk around the lovely surrounding area briefly before we headed back to the ranch. Back in the car we continued our conversation.

Ed, sitting in the front seat with her, asked, "Can you explain to us what all this intimidation and threats from these mysterious people is all about? This has us really worried. I don't like being shot at or assaulted., especially when we can't get help from the police."

Ada, keeping her eyes strictly on the road, replied, "All I know is that Ahmed has owned many kinds of businesses over the years, most of them with European and some Asian connections, though he's long since been a naturalized American citizen. And as you know, recent events in the Middle East have made it difficult, even hazardous, for many Americans to do business in some of those areas. Ahmed won't give me any details, but he's told me that operatives of one foreign government once threatened him and his family if he tries to reclaim property they have confiscated from him. He won't tell me which country or anything more than that. Apparently these people are determined to shut him up."

"And you think this may be behind these gangland-like experiences we've been having lately?" I asked.

"I would guess so. But, frankly, I'm scared. I wish I could get him to turn over this whole business to the police, but he won't have that. He says any notoriety could ruin his businesses abroad. I guess we have to just take one day at a time and hope that he knows what he is doing."

Ed looked back over his shoulder at me in the back seat and flicked me a set of raised eyebrows. I could only shrug my shoulders in reply.

In another half hour we were back at the damaged ranch gate. We drove past several men who were busy repairing and reinforcing it, on up the hill and into the carport.

We thanked Ada for a delightful interlude and lunch, gave one another hugs, and went into the house for a little siesta. It was now quite late in the afternoon, and we were wondering uneasily how Sin-Bed was making out with his enforced meeting with the hoods who had called on the phone.

We didn't have to wait long to find out.

That November Stinging Rebuke

Ed reports. . .

The morning after our date with Ada, and after Sin-Bed's late night return from his mysterious city rendezvous, he called the two of us into his now restored office. He asked us to sit down while he completed some papers he was working with on his desk.

Finished, he turned to us and abruptly said, "I'm going to have to make a trip to Europe very soon. My wife will go with me to Switzerland where our youngest son is in school. We will spend the Holidays there with him. The season is now almost upon us and I probably won't return until well after the first of the year.

"However, because I already have invitations out for our scheduled annual fall harvest party in a couple of weeks, I can't leave until after that. During my absence Miss Longstreet will be in charge here, though she will not attend the party. She will be with her family over in Utah through the Holidays.

"My wife will be coming to the ranch a day or two before the party just to check and see that everything is in order. Two of our sons will be with her to help with the party, also. And I want to remind you, Jackie, to take extra precautions to see that there are no bobby pins or stray hairs in the bathrooms. Check the chair and couch cushions carefully." I raised a mental eyebrow at this, but he was still expounding.

"We always have this yearly affair catered with the same people, so they are familiar with our routine and what is expected of them. All the food, wines, tables, dishes and other things for the party are provided by the caterer. You two, along with our sons, may help with arriving guests.

"You will have a prepared list of invited guests which you will check off as they arrive. Make a note of anyone who apparently should not be there. I have hired a private security firm to provide us with three of their officers to attend and cover our party. Report any person to them whom you feel should not be here.

"It also might be a good idea, before the party begins, for you, Ed, to make another perimeter patrol with the truck, just to see that our fences and gates are all intact. We expect about 150 people to attend." I felt an inner chill.

He gave me that stare. " Do you have any questions?"

I said, "Yes, one. I've noticed that we have had an extraordi-

nary number of yellow jackets or so-called meat bees around here
this fall. I've already been stung once myself. They breed in the
ground all over this area, and I think we should immediately try to
eradicate as many of their nests as possible, and also set up a number of traps around the lawn area where the party will be held.
They're a terrible pest and can be a serious problem, especially if a
guest were to get stung and has an allergic reaction to the sting.
They sometimes can be lethal."

Sin-Bed nodded and told me to get what I needed. I wanted
to ask him how his meeting with his irate telephone caller had
gone the previous night, but decided that I'd better forget it. We
would probably find out later from Ada after she returned from
her Utah holiday vacation with her sons.

The next ten days or so went by with no further hostile activity by anyone. I spent considerable time spraying yellow jacket
nests in the ground, and mounting more than a dozen bee traps,
baited with a special pheromone attractant, in the trees and shrubs
around the yard. In two days I had captured more than 500 of the
pests in these traps. I reported this to Sin-Bed who simply said,
"Good." Thereafter he spent most of his time in his city office
getting ready for his trip. Ada was also away working in town at
her office before her own journey.

With less than four days before the big party, I was busy
mowing the nearly acre of lawn, and preening and pruning plants
and shrubs around the pool, getting ready for the caterers to set
up their tables and all the rest of their stuff, including colored
lights, linen table cloths, chafing dishes, a lot of silver and crystal, tiki torches and other party paraphenalia. Jackie was working frantically to get the entire house cleaned and ready for the
onslaught of guests.

The day before the party, Sin-Bed's wife, Maria Disrahlbi and
her two older sons, with dates, arrived to spend the night and to
get things ready to greet her guests. We met them as they got out
of their Lincoln town car, and introduced ourselves.

"Ahmed has told me so much about you two," Maria said,

extending us a plump hand and bright smile. "It's a pleasure finally to meet you both."

Maria, we discovered, was a very pleasant, really lovely latino woman of middle age. She displayed a flawless complexion, dark eyes, sleek black hair drawn back in a bun, and a bright affable smile. She was also, as Ada had mentioned, very much overweight. Her two sons, Tom and Edward, both husky young men in their twenties, attending with their respective dates, proved cheerful and helpful as we got things under way for the party.

The day for the big Autumn Festival, as Sin-Bed called it, finally arrived, bright, sunny and beautifully mild. The caterer's were on time, and food and drink were already assembled in the large kitchen. The tables, linen, silver chafing dishes and all the other party accoutrements were installed and ready.

Sin-Bed arrived from the The City early in the morning and Maria greeted him warmly with a big kiss and a hug as he got out of his car. They went, arm in arm, into the house.

The party was scheduled to begin at three o'clock, and Jackie and I were ready with our guest list at the garden entrance. She had been wearing an afternoon dress with an crisp white apron until Maria noticed it and asked her why she was wearing it.

"No," she said, almost like a mother, " Please take it off. We want you and Ed to be our guests today. Remember, this party is fully catered. You have nothing to do but enjoy yourselves." We were amazed at her generosity and thanked her profusely.

In going over the guests' names we were intrigued to see all the high-powered citizens invited. There were three ambassadors, half a dozen consuls from different countries, a university president, and a number of distinguished professors and writers, some well-known in the City's newspapers, all with either spouses or companions. It would be quite an assembly.

We now had a chance to see Sin-Bed in his full splendor, calling ambassadors and political leaders by their first names, kissing the hands of their ladies, and generally playing the delighted host.

Maria and sons with their dates stood beside him in the receiving line, beaming at all the guests as they arrived.

I couldn't help but think about Ada who was not with us, and who had met Sin-Bed as a guest at this very party years earlier. I wondered what she was thinking at this moment.

By five o'clock the food lines were well under way and guests were seating themselves at the more than twenty-five large tables elegantly assembled around the lawn. The sun was getting lower in the sky and the caterers turned on several strings of Japanese lanterns which gave the entire area a warm, lush glow. I decided to get the insect repellent torches fired up. I circled the party site with a lighter, igniting more than twenty tiki-type torches, adding to the warmth of the scene.

I scanned the whole party area, looking for anything that might disturb the magic of the moment. It was, indeed, a memorable and elegant event, though I noted one or two people swatting at some kind of a bug around their food. Other than that, the scene was perfect.

Everyone had now been seated for a while, and most of their filet and rack of lamb and other goodies had been served and consumed. With dessert now being served, Sin-Bed, resplendent in a white dinner jacket and cummerbund, arose to offer a champagne toast to his guests, all of whom had already had their flute glasses filled for that moment.

"Good friends," he began, raising his glass, "I want to thank you for coming to share this festive annual occasion with me and my family, I..."

At that instant a woman at a table across from him shrieked, stood up abruptly, and began swatting at something under her skirt. A second later, another woman at the same table screamed, and in getting up, upset the entire table. Glasses, dishes, chafing dishes, food, champagne and purses all went to the ground. In less than a minute four or five other women in the same area began screeching and swatting things under their dresses. Sin -Bed, still holding his champagne glass frozen in mid-air, stared unbelievingly at the chaos.

Those godamn bees, I thought! I had set up all of those traps two days before, and had caught hundreds of the critters, which I had shown to Sin-Bed, but the attractant in the traps seemed to have attracted even more of them to the area.

It looked as if the problem table had been set up right over undetected nests in the lawn. One of the upset ladies had apparently put her shoe heel directly into a hidden nest hole. Dozens of the stinging pests were now buzzing and circling the tables, producing a bedlam of swinging arms, shouts and screams. In less than five minutes the whole lawn area was pandemonium, with both men and women swatting and yelling at the angry, fiercely stinging insects.

I then remembered that yellow jackets can sting their victims more than once, which makes their assault inifinitely worse than the sting of the honey bee whose stinger becomes imbedded in his victim's skin, thus killing it. Not so with the "meat bee," the yellow jacket.

By now both men and women all over the entire lawn dinner area were screaming, swatting wildly, and weeping; men were cursing. Three elegantly attired women jumped into the shallow end of the adjacent pool with their clothes on to get away from the assault.

Sin-Bed, totally unstrung by it all, now yelled for me to "get in there and kill those #@*^% bugs." It was the first time I had ever heard him use profanity. But there was little Jackie and I could do but help people who had been stung to their cars and offer first aid for their stings.

All in all we later guessed than not less than thirty of his guests had been assaulted, with the rest of the assemblage feeling everything from hysterical amusement to outrage. Fortunately, most of the guests had already finished their meal and were in the middle of Sin-Bed's toast when all hell broke loose.

Of course, the story of the "Festival" debacle made all the next-day papers, and Sin-Bed spent most of the next couple of days offering apologies and writing notes of contrition to all his guests. It had become almost an international incident.

He was scheduled to leave for his European trip the following week, and called us both into his office the day before he left. He never mentioned the bee disaster, but thanked us for our service to him and his family, and apologized to us for the upset we had been through with our "invaders" and the phone calls. Apparently Ada had clued him in to our concerns.

"I expect my trip will resolve the problems with these trouble-makers," he said. "In the meantime, while I'm gone, I trust you will take good care of this place. Remember, Miss Longstreet will be here much of the time to help keep my work here on schedule. She has told me how much she likes you both, and I'm sure you will get along well. I don't yet know when I'll be back, but it may be late in January."

"We'll be just fine, sir," I said. "We hope you have a nice trip and holiday." We wondered why he never referred to Ada by her first name. She was always "Miss Longstreet." Apparently just one of his European idiosyncracies.

Thanksgiving and Christmas were now almost upon us. But before Sin-Bed left we asked him if we could have our children with us at the ranch over the Holidays.

He gave us a cold studied glare.

"How old are they," he asked with a frown.

"They're all grown, and we have four grandchildren," Jackie said. "They're all responsible people. We will take extra care to see that everything here is well taken care of and your privacy is not invaded."

Sin-Bed, still frowning, after an extended pause, finally said, "All right. But it's against my better judgment. I've never allowed any of my other help have families here in my absence, but I guess you'll be okay." He paused, thought a moment, then said, " You may have the west wing of bedrooms for your family. My office will be locked during my absence, and you are not to enter it for any reason," he said. He gave us another of his his patented steely stares but said, "Go ahead and enjoy yourselves."

He left on schedule, five of our kids and three grandchildren came to enjoy the holidays on the big ranch, and everyone had a splendid time. Even Butch and the cats were happy.

Ada had been with her grown children and grandchildren in Utah over the Holidays, and at the end of the first week of the new year she arrived at the ranch with a big hug for both of us. We told her about the lawn party fiasco, and she nearly collapsed laughing.

"'Oh, poor Ahmed. He must have died," she giggled. "I wish I had been here."

During the next couple of weeks our days melded into a regular routine. Jackie worked hard in the house; I did the pool, the yard and landscape work. Ada came out from the City on weekends, and took us several times to others of her favorite watering holes and dinner houses, including twice at the internationally famous Silverado County Club on the storied Silverado Trail of Napa County. She had become a delightful companion while at the ranch, and a good generous friend. We even had dinner one evening at her home in a nearby town. It was a lovely place, with a sparkling pool and extensive beautifully maintained gardens.

By the last week of January we still had not heard from Sin-Bed as to when he might be returning, nor had Ada. Then one morning we got a call from our long-lost buddies, Joan and Bob Renney. We had had occasional phone conversations with them over the passing weeks, but it had been months since we had seen them. They wanted to come by and get caught up, so we made arrangements for them to come that coming week-end when Ada could also be there to meet them. We had told her so much about them, we were sure she would like to meet another pair of gutsy geezers like us, the one's who had gotten us into this fantasy world to begin with.

Joan and Bob breezed up the ranch road in their Lexus and greeted us with shouts and hugs. Ada came out and also hugged them both as if they had been friends for years. We all went into the big living room, settled down and began another recap of our respective recent lives.

Joan said, "I've got some exciting news. Bob and I are going to

Italy next month for our vacation."

"Italy!" we exclaimed, "Where did this idea come from?"

"Well," Joan said, "Bob and I have always been students of Italian culture, and we thought, with the Langstons—our employers, you may remember—being gone also for a time, that it would be a great time to make the trip."

Ada mentioned that she and Sin-Bed has been to Italy several times and loved every visit, especially the Florence area. She asked what part of the country they were going to.

"We like the northern part, from Turin up into the Lake country in the Alps. We'll probably take a small villa there for three weeks or so," Bob explained.

After some cocktails and hors d'oevres, Joan said, "We're also thinking of possibly quitting this lifestyle. It's been over eight years now, and we've put away quite a bit of money. We may decide to open our own business which would be catering fresh organic vegetables to some of our more posh specialty restaurants in the area and in the City. We just need to find the right property at the right price."

Bob interjected, "If we do decide to quit when we get back from Italy we wondered if you guys would be interested in taking over our jobs with the Langstons. You know they pay very well and are hardly ever there."

Jackie and I looked at each other, Ada looked startled, and all we could say for the moment was, "Wow!"

"And from what you have told us in your letters about being shot at and broken into up here, we don't think this is a very safe job for you two. We sure wouldn't put up with it," feisty Joan said.

Ada looked stunned, then said, "I'm afraid I'll have to agree with you there. I've told Ed and Jackie that I was concerned about them here, too." She looked over at us. "I know Ahmed will die if he comes home and finds that you're considering leaving here. He has become very dependent upon you two."

"Well," I said. "We'd have to think over something like this." I looked at Ada and commented, "You know, Ada, Ahmed has been good to us while we've been here, but he's not exactly generous with his money."

Bob chimed in with, "On our recommendation the Langstons would probably be willing to pay you fifty percent more than what you've told us you're getting here. After more than five years with them we get considerably more than that."

Jackie and I looked at each other. "We'll have to do a lot of thinking about this. But it sounds interesting," I said.

After some more reminiscing they gave us hugs and headed back to their Langston lair roughly seventy miles away over the hills in the northern Sonoma Valley.

Ada and the two of us watched as their car wended its way down the winding mountain road to the valley.

She turned to us and said, a bit wistfully, "I have the feeling that today may be another turning point in your lives. I think Ahmed might be willing to give you a substantial raise, but you'd better check into this other possibility too."

Tears welled up in her eyes "I love you both," she whispered, with almost frantic hugs for each of us. The very next morning we had a phone call from Sin-Bed in Switzerland telling us that he would be returning within two weeks via San Francisco, and to tell Ada. Ada was right. It was indeed to be another turning point in our peripatetic lives. Those weeks prior to Sin-Bed's return were frenetic with making sure everything was neat, clean, and in the right place. Jackie and I had had several changes of mind on the Langston situation, but felt we should at least go over to their place if the opportunity really came, look it over, and talk with them.

Joan and Bob called on the Monday of the week Sin-Bed was to return and said they had given the Langstons notice. They would take their Italian vacation and then leave. And were we now interested in taking over their jobs?

We said we were interested but would need to look over the place and talk with them first. We had learned a lot about these kinds of jobs after working for Loony Lulu and Sin-Bed, and wanted to cover every angle before committing ourselves on anything. Of course money was primary in our needs. It was why we were in this bizarre lifestyle in the first place.

Joan and Bob made an appointment for us to meet the Langstons the day before Sin-Bed was due to be back at the ranch. We had a rather solemn talk with Ada about the opportunity. But she urged us to take the job if it really met our needs. "God, how I'll miss you two if you leave us. But you should do what you both need at this time in your lives," she said just before we left for our talk with the Langstons.

The Langston Lure

Ed reports. . .

We had seen many pictures of the Langston's place from Bob and Joan, but we were really blown away when we first drove into their estate not far from legendary author Jack London's fabled home in the Valley of the Moon, one of Sonoma County's best known landmarks.

The entrance to the place was, surprisingly, through a wide open gate. There seemed to be no visible security precautions anywhere, at least by the entrance. The huge house, of soft-textured fieldstone, only one of several Langston homes scattered across the country, was set in the middle of more than two hundred acres of spectacular landscapes. There were orchards and pastures, vineyards and tennis courts with spectator galleries, a huge swimming pool and lovely adjacent pool house, plus another small lake with a dancing fountain. Acres and acres of both flower and vegetable gardens seemed to be everywhere.

There were separate corrals, pastures, and barns for Tennessee walking horses, storage barns for hay and feed, and a huge separate fieldstone building which had once been used as a winery, now containing some of the Langston's collection of antique cars and motorcycles. There was a helipad and a separate hanger for their

helicopter, fruit processing and packing sheds, and seemingly endless rows of both wine and table grapes. Crowning this whole landscape were tens of thousands of tulips, daffodils, and narcissus,
now beginning their massive early spring display.

We were stunned at the beauty of it all as we drove up to the
five-car garage and carports near the helipad. Bob and Joan raced
out of the back kitchen door with their usual exhuberant enthusiasm with hugs and kisses all around.

"Come on in. I'll show you where we've been living for nearly
six years. Let's do a tour of the house," Joan bubbled with Bob
grinning happily in the background. Four of the Langston's me-
nagerie of dogs bounded happily around us, bellowing greetings.

"They never bite, but they sure let us know when anyone's
coming into the place," Joan said. "I just love 'em all." Just then
we heard a cat or cats meowing and saw three of them up on the
patio roof by the kitchen door all hollering at the same time.

"They're hungry, as usual," Joan said. "We'll feed them and
the dogs when we get through with our house tour. That'll be part
of your chores if you come here. The Langstons are expecting to be
here this afternoon to meet you, but are leaving in a couple of
weeks for a three weeks' tour of the Mediterranean, so we'll have
plenty of time to look around after they leave. After lunch we can
take a drive around the place. "

We followed Bob and Joan into the kitchen door and took a
whirlwind tour of the entire fabulous house. Because Jackie would
be doing cooking with this job, she was anxious to check out the
kitchen and all of its facilities. She found it amazing. There were
two huge double-door refrigerators, a sorbet making machine, a
walk-in freezer in an adjacent pantry, a massive six-burner Wolf
commercial gas range, two dishwashers, and an enormous pantry
full of exquisite silver, crystal and dinnerware. The kitchen floor
was of slate flagstone.

Jackie kept shaking her head in amazement. "I don't know
about this, Joan. I've never cooked on a monster like this stove. It's
scary."

"It's a breeze, Jackie. Easier than your home stove. Much better control over your cooking, too. Really, it won't take long to get used to it at all."

Jackie looked at me with a look of near panic. I said with as much tenderness as I could muster, "It's just a stove, honey, with on and off knobs just like the ones at home. You'll do fine. I just wonder how I'll make out as a butler here."

Bob said, " You guys will be great. Remember these people are hardly ever here. It's mainly a caretaking job. And you'll have all kinds of help in your outside work. After we get through the house tour I want you to meet Frank Bartoloman, our field supervisor. He's a neat guy, and I know you'll like him.

"About all I've had to do here is do simple maintenance work like touch-up painting and an occasional bout with a leaky faucet. Frank supervises a number of field hands and and maintains the extensive orchards and plantings you see everywhere. He also knows a lot of personal stuff about the Langstons. He's a fascinating story-teller. "

After a quick tour of the ground floor of the house, the Langstons arrived earlier than expected. We were interviewed quite briefly in their gorgeous sunny main lounge which was filled with exquisite floral accented furniture, much of it antique, with matching drapes covering floor-to-ceiling French windows. An imported hand carved mantel surmounted a white marble fireplace across from an entire wall of massive bookcases. Memorabilia from many overseas trips covered a number of marble-topped tables. It was a truly magnificent room.

D'Arcy Langston entered as all of us rose to meet her. She was a tall, darkly pretty woman, we guessed about fifty, immaculately dressed, apparently ready both to meet us and also leave quickly to get ready for their trip. Bob and Joan earlier had told us a lot about both of them.

She was the daughter of a former high State Department official, attended several European girls' schools, finally graduating from one of them with minimum distinction, courtesy of her father's financial influence on the school's board of trustees. Her marriage to George Langston was her fourth, having produced two sons and two daughters, one child with each of her four marriages, all of them to wealthy men.

Bob and Joan also had mentioned that she relentlessly pursued publicity in The City's society columns and relished being photographed with visiting pseudo-royalty and show-business types. If she wasn't contacted by society editors at least once a week, she would call them herself with tales of real or fancied recent experiences. A telephone addict, Joan reported that she spends hours every day regaling friends with the latest gossip. According to Joan, it had been widely speculated that D'Arcy has had numerous sub-rosa affairs with other men in her tomcat society's circle.

She gave each of us a quick cool smile, shook hands and told us that Bob and Joan had already given them so much information about us that she really didn"t need to get into our backgrounds or qualifications.

"Today, Mr. Langston and I would really like to know if you are interested in taking over here from Joan and Bob. They've been with us now for nearly six years, and we hate to see them go. But do you think you could be comfortable here?"

Just then George Langston entered the room, quickly shook hands with us and lit a cigarette. Dressed in a casual pullover sweater and chino pants he came across as a stocky man of medium height, with a somewhat dark complexion, balding, with deep-set restless eyes which continuously darted around the room.

"We'd like to discuss our responsibilities, your pay scale, and what you expect of us before we make a commitment, Mrs. Langston," Jackie said. "Remember, I'm not a Cordon Blu trained cook as Joan is. I. . ."

D'Arcy interruped with a waved hand and said, "I'm sure you'll do fine. Joan has told me of the many good things you have done in the kitchen. Our tastes in cooking are really quite simple. Right, George?" She was clearly anxious to leave and get ready for their trip.

"Right," George echoed as D'Arcy reached over to him and

snatched his burning cigarette from his fingers.

"We don't need that nasty smoke in here now, George." She snuffed it out in a nearby ashtray. George shrugged and smiled an annoyed smirk.

After several more minutes of small talk, we made an appointment to return the following week with a final answer and a more thorough discussion of what our work would be.

The Langstons left in George's new Ferrari as Joan and Bob walked us out to our car.

"Well, what did you think of them?" Joan asked, looking at us both expectantly.

"I'd say you described them both very accurately," I said. Jackie nodded her agreement."They aren't exactly the cuddly types," I added. "I guess we've been spoiled by our relationship with Ada Longstreet." I moved towards the back kitchen door and the car.

Joan said, "Wait, before you go, let's have a quick look at the upstairs part of the house. It will give you a little idea of their lifestyle. It's fabulous."

We went up elegantly curved stairs flanked with a fluted ballustrade, to a long, broad hallway which led to six large bedrooms, each with its own bath, each furnished with a different but elegant touch. Many of the furniture pieces were clearly antiques of considerable value.

Joan led us through two exquisitely paneled double doors into the master suite, a masterpiece of interior decor. There was a huge king-sized, canopied bed which faced a lovely fireplace with imported tiles on the hearth and facia. Bookcases covered one wall, with several marble-topped tables, each covered with expensive bric-a-brac, scattered around the huge room. Prints and photographs taken on their many foreign trips covered other walls.

"Come in here, Jackie. I want you to see how 'a woman of culture' dresses." Joan beckoned to us to follow her into an adjacent room. It actually was an enormous walk-in closet, probably 15 by 30 feet with rack after rack of expensive womens' clothes of every conceivable kind hanging along both sides of the room. We noted that many of the dresses still had price tags dangling from sleeves. D'Arcy apparently was an impulse shopper. Then another built-in cedar-lined cabinet opened to show more than a dozen fur coats from chinchilla and sable to ermine, fox, and mink.

Overhead a large skylight brought in a flood of soft north light, giving the whole room an almost ethereal illumination. D'Arcy's glass-covered built-in dressing table covered an entire end wall of the room. Innumerable mini-bottles and flasks of perfume and other cosmetics covered the mirrored top. At the other end of this mega-dressing room was another floor-to-ceiling closet filled with shelf after shelf of just sweaters, each neatly boxed in a transparent container. There must have been more than fifty, each with a de-signer sweater inside.

Jackie asked Joan if she were responsible for taking care of all these clothes.

"No, though I do voluntarily sometimes do some ironing for her for some special occasion. She usually sends out laundry and dry cleaning to a company which comes by on a regular schedule."

Jackie shook her head, saying, " I just can't imagine how any one person could ever wear so many clothes. I've always lived by the rule that when you buy something new, you get rid of some-thing else."

Joan then reminded us that these clothes of D'Arcy's were just a small sample of her wardrobe. "Don't forget that D'Arcy and George also have several other homes scattered all over the coun-try. She, and George too, have similar separate wardrobes in each of their homes. Remember, this place is just a week-end haunt. Their main place is in San Francisco in the posh Pacific Heights part of town."

The whole place momentarily had developed in me a strange sense of unreality. Was all this real? Were these people real? And at this point were *we* real? It was now pinch-me time. I did—and it was, all of it, real.

We all then made our way back down the stairs to the entry

foyer, out to the front portico, thence slowly out to where our car was parked near the five-car garage.

Bob mentioned that he wanted us to meet Frank Bartoloman, the ranch field supervisor, before we left. "Frank's one of the most helpful and knowledgeable men in his field I've ever met." Bob led us all over to the rear of the house where Frank was just finishing up a transplant job on several fruit trees. He waved at us with a broad smile, and approached, wiping his hands on a red bandana he wore casually around his neck. Bob introduced us, saying that if we ever needed to know anything about the ranch—anything— Bob emphasized the word—Frank was the man to see. Joan had already told us of his stories of a few wild happenings on the premises in recent years, mostly involving D'Arcy and her swinging friends.

We got a picture of a strikingly handsome man, about 38 to 40, lean, tall and muscular, with a thick mane of chestnut very wavy hair, bright blue eyes, and a deep tan, especially on his lower arms which were constantly exposed to the sun. He wore a broad-brimmed western stockman's hat on the back of his head as if he had been born with it. He laughed easily and seemed to be completely comfortable with anyone he was with. Though we was married, and had several children, we could see how he could be an amorous magnet for some of D'Arcy's randy and predatory female breakfast buddies.

We shook hands and Frank offered to drive us around the property for a once-over before we left. We declined the offer, feeling that we had to get back to the details of closing down our Sin-Bed job, and told him we'd take a rain check.

We waved goodbye and told Bob and Joan we'd be in touch very shortly.

That evening Ada welcomed us back to the ranch with obvious anxiety. We all went into the big living room for a brief conference.

"Well, what have you decided; are you leaving us?" Her voice clearly reflected concern.

I looked at Jackie who gave me a little nod, and replied, "Yes, we think we should grab the opportunity, though we haven't committed ourselves yet. We will go for another visit and a longer talk next week. I suspect we will make our final decision then. But mentally I guess we have accepted the job."

Jackie added, " From what Bob and Joan tell us, we can expect a pay check with the Langstons more than double what Mr. Disrahlbi's been giving us here. We'll know for sure next week."

Ada stood up, looked at both of us with clear glances of affection, saying,

"I know Ahmed will be very upset if you leave. But I think you are both doing what is probably best for you. After all, you got into this bizarre lifestyle to bail yourselves out of financial disaster. It looks as if fate has aimed you in the right direction." She tearfully gave us each a strong, long hug and went back to her room.

Sin-Bed was due back in The City the following day but we got a phone call from London saying that he was remaining there for another week.

Good. This gave us even more time to get ready for our coming move. Ada also already began scouting around for someone to replace us.

The following week we had our second meeting with the Langstons, confirmed our sharply upgraded salaries, and made arrangements to begin with them before they left from their planned Mediterranean cruise. Bob and Joan would also leave at the same time. All we had to do now was face Sin-Bed.

He arrived right on time after his London stop-over, and seemed brimming with unaccustomed cheerfulness as he climbed out of his Mercedes on a sunny morning. Ada had met him at the airport and brought him out to the ranch.

I helped him with his luggage as he said over his shoulder, "Ed and Jackie, give me a few hours to settle back in here, then we'll have a chance to get caught up. It's great getting back home."

Ada gave us kind of a frozen smile as she went with him into the house. Apparently she hadn't told him yet of our plans to leave.

Late that afternoon Sin-Bed called us into his office where Ada was waiting with him. It was clear from his expression that she had finally told him of our decision.

"Miss Longstreet has just told me of your plans to go to another job. Frankly, I'm stunned. I had no idea you were unhappy here," he said, frowning. He was almost into a sulk.

Jackie replied, "No, Mr. Disrahlbi, it's not that we are unhappy here. Quite the opposite. But we must take what little working time we have left in our lives to earn as much as possible, and this offer from the Langstons is, well, it's just too good to turn down. I really. . ." He interrupted her.

"Just how much are these people paying you?" he asked. That trade-mark intimidating stare was back, aimed directly at me.

"Almost exactly double what we are getting here, sir, plus quite a liberal work schedule," I said. "But, really, we have been quite happy here for nearly a year, but had hoped for a substantial raise. It hasn't come, Mr. Disrahlbi, and we feel we simply cannot afford at our advanced ages doing hard physical work every day, to go on this way indefinitely.

"Even more important, living here with these mysterious phone calls, house assaults, and gunshots—well, we feel we should take advantage of an opportunity where we can both sharply enhance our income and at the same time eliminate this kind of continuing and growing uneasiness that we've had here."

Sin-Bed and Ada both were quietly looking at the floor, seemingly in a momentary funk. He drummed a pencil on his desk. Finally Ada said,

"I've already told you of how fond of you we have become. We will. . ."

Sin-Bed interrupted again. "Yes, we have found both of you a great asset to our property and work here at the ranch." He abruptly changed the subject momentarily, asking again, "Just how much are these Langston people going to pay you?"

"Three thousand dollars a month, a four-room furnished apartment, all food and needed clothing, plus medical and dental benefits, with an expected raise, if we work out, of another $500 monthly after six months."

Sin-Bed seemed stunned. "Well," he said, shaking his head, "I can't match that offer. I'm already paying you two more than I ever have paid anyone else to work out here. So I guess we will have to make other arrangements. Miss Longstreet, I know, will also miss you both very much." He looked over at Ada, now furtively dabbing at her eyes with a handkerchief. She nodded, then burst fully into tears.

"Just when were you planning to leave us?" Sin-Bed asked us. I explained about the Langston's planned brief absence for their cruise, and mentioned that our friends Bob and Joan also were leaving them at the same time.

We all rose, and we shook hands with Sin-Bed . He would never hug anyone, especially an employee. But we gave quick hugs to Ada, and quietly went back to our cottage.

The new die was now cast.

Jackie reports. . .

The next week or so in memory is a blur. We made a 400-mile hurried round trip home to check on things, with our big house still not sold, got caught up on our local news, then returned to the ranch and Ada for a more formal goodbye.

We drove up to the ranch gate and phoned the house for the gate release. Ada answered. "Oh, great! You're home!" she exclaimed, clearly happy to have us back, even for just a visit. It almost did feel like coming home. We drove up the winding grade that was now so familiar, into the carport, and walked through the house gate where Ada threw her arms open and nearly crushed us both with affectionate hugs.

Once seated in the big living room, Ada said that Ahmed would not be at the ranch during our visit, but sent his best wishes to us. She still had not been able to find a replacement for us, but had hopes of hiring a couple who had previously worked at her office in The City.

We told her of our trip home and our very mixed feelings about moving over to the Langstons.

"I'm sure you'll do just as well over there as you have here with us," she said quietly. "But I have missed you both terribly already." Tears welled into her eyes as she fumbled for a tissue in her purse.

I said, "Ada, we will never forget your kindness and concern. We know we have made a new life-long friend, and we will report in to you regularly as to how we're doing." We hugged for what seemed like ten minutes.

Then, after a bit more of heartfelt reminiscing, we rose and went into our cottage to retrieve the last of our belongings. We waved a teary goodbye, and in the mirror watched Ada giving us a "thumbs up" as we disappeared down the grade into the valley. We would truly miss that lady. Little did we know just how much.

CHAPTER 5

Langstonitis

Ed reports. . .

Our first week at the Langstons' place is almost another blur in memory because of our need to carefully check out everything on our duties list before we actually got into our new routines. But our new small apartment over the garage was comfortable, and we had several days to settle in before the Langstons came to the place for a last-minute conference prior to their impending Mediterranean trip. Joan and Bob had now left for Italy, and had left us pages of helpful instructions about the place, locations of certain things in various parts of the enormous house, and suggestions for handling possible problems, one of which, totally unexpected, was about to land on us.

D'Arcy and George breezed in one afternoon, having first called to advise us that they would not be there overnight and not to expect them for meals. They just wanted to double check with us on things we needed to know before they left on their trip.

We met them as they rumbled up in George's red Ferrari, then got out and walked into the house with us. D'Arcy did most of the talking, something we discovered later was her characteristic way of controlling any situation. Just grab on to the conversation and then never let go.

"Ed and Jackie, we have some news for you that we didn't know when we first talked, but I think you'll find it of interest. Joan and Bob may have told you something about our son, Gregory. He's now fifteen, and will be coming here to stay with you while we're on our cruise and in Europe. Although he has had his troubles in school, I think you'll like him. We know you'll get along famously." Jackie's mouth was open in disbelief, clearly absolutely stunned at her news.

Certainly it had not been in our agreement to be responsible for the care and supervision of children, let alone a boy whose wild reputation had already preceded him in three different prep schools from which he had been expelled.

"Mrs. Langston," I said. "We cannot be responsible for the supervision or care of your son. This was not in our agreement or job description when we agreed to come here and take over for Bob and Joan. We simply. . ."

D'Arcy broke in with a curt wave of her hand, and said bluntly, "I'm sorry, but we didn't know at the time we first talked with you, that Gregory would be leaving his school and coming here. I'm afraid this is the way things will have to be, at least until we get back from our trip. We've enrolled him in our local school here for the balance of the spring semester and I think he will fit in there very well. He used to know some of the kids there when he lived here with us here several years ago. Really, I think when you get to know each other you'll all get along fine." She flicked the ash from her cigarette, and seemed also to flick us a half-sneer that clearly said, "Gotcha"!

After giving us a few more bits of information concerning housekeeping, the names of local law enforcement and fire prevention people, and the names and phone numbers of her dogs' veterinarians, and her lawyer, the two of them roared off with little but a cursory wave of the hand. George had said absolutely nothing during their hurried visit. We began already to get the Langston picture. God, how we suddenly missed Ada.

Being in shock from this news would take a couple of days to wear off, and it did nothing but firm up our initial uneasiness about this new assignment. We had heard so much about this kid

from Joan and Bob, all of it negative, that we were now prepared—
or, rather, unprepared, for almost anything.

Three days later D'Arcy drove in with young Greg , staying
just long enough to dump his luggage and introduce us to him,
telling him and us that "we were the boss" while she and George
were gone. He greeted us with a limp hand shake and wise-guy
sneer, and never looked directly at either of us. He turned away
before we had even had a chance to acknowledge the introduction.

Oh, sure, I thought, we were going to be the boss of this kid as
we watched him walk with a cocky gait up to his second floor
room. I was developing a prickly feeling at the back of my neck. It
already was also clear that there was absolutely no affection shown
between mother and son. Plain, poorly masked hostility was more
like it.

We immediately got a picture of a loud, red-haired, freckle-
faced, sneering bundle of contradictions, of medium height, well
built for his fifteen years, looking older than his age, superficially
charming, but a kid used to doing what he wants whenever he
wants. Bob and Joan had mentioned that he was a gun nut and
already had built a reputation as an out-of-control kid at all three
schools he had attended within the past three years. As psycholo-
gists and counselors, Jackie and I now had a closeup look at a true
budding teenage sociopath.

We didn't have long to wait for the first problem.

The first couple days with Greg were pretty much without
incident. Jackie got meals, Greg used his bike to tool off to friends'
places (as far as we knew), Jackie got used to the new big stove and
began to have some fun exploring the amazing collections of
dishware, silver, and crystal in D'Arcy's supersized pantries. I got
acquainted with the place's tool sheds, barns and got introduced
by Frank Bartoloman to some of the field hands working the place.

But at the end of his first week with us Jackie got the jolt of
her life when she went up to Greg's room and discovered its walls
blasted with splashes and blotches of paint from floor to ceiling.
The whole room was a splotched multi-color mess, and on return-

ing to our quarters later she discovered he had blasted the sides of our garage apartment with paint balls as well.

D'Arcy and George wouldn't let him have a .22 rifle, but she had given in to his constant badgering and got him a paintball gun set. The little air-powered gun shoots pellets of paint in dozens of colors, which explode on impact making a monumental mess. We found out later that he had joined a local "junior militia" which was made up of other wealthy kids and their families, who went out into the woods on actual "combat" patrols, shooting paint balls at one another. "Casualties" were duly recorded and awards given to the "infantryman" with the most paintball hits on the "enemy."

Apparently he had let his underlying hostility to any authority have free reign with "practicing" with his paintball gun on the walls of his own room, and anything else within range, including our quarters.

Jackie called me in from the back of the property to tell me what he had done, saying that we'd better have a "who's boss" conference and confiscate his "weapon" before any more damage was done.

I put away my yard tools and marched up to his room. I knocked on his closed door, got a loud "Come in," and found him on his paint-spattered bed, banging away on a battered guitar and screeching out a top-ten rock tune. But as I opened the door he simultaneously tossed his guitar to the floor and threw a handful of his paint balls at me. Several broke and splattered my shirt.

The kid roared with laughter, pointing at me and telling me what a great target I had been. "I couldn't miss—all I had to do was aim at the door when you opened it," he gasped through his chuckles.

I was filled with a sudden desire to flip this kid with a little karate I had learned in the service, but kept my temper, trying at the same time to use my training as a psychologist to remind myself of a few things. Here was a kid who had had very little TLC in his early life, who is filled with raging hostility, and who probably had never had any adult give him anything but total indifference or harsh abuse, let alone any love or concern. We had been through the teen crises with all seven of our own kids, and I understood a lot of what was driving Greg. But being a parent was one thing; being a temporary—and unwilling—surrogate was quite different.

"Greg, you're a jerk," was all I could think of to say as I wiped down my shirt with a wet towel from his adjacent bathroom. Fortunately, the paints he was messing with were water soluble and would wash out, but that wasn't the point.

"Your days as a paintball infantryman are over." I said. I walked over to his desk which was piled high with assorted debris, all of it covered with splotches of paint, reached across the pile and picked up his paint gun and a couple of boxes of his "ammunition."

"This stuff is going into hibernation," I snapped. "You clearly don't give a damn about anyone or anything but yourself. You have proved that you have the sense of responsibility of a two-year-old. You will get to use this stuff from here on out *only* out in the woods on your so-called militia grounds.

"Now, the first thing you're going to do is come out to our place and clean off all the paint you've shot all over it. Then you're coming back here with a bucket, sponge, soap and water, and get every damned bit of this crud off your own room and everything in it. You also will wash every bit of clothing you've smeared up, then iron it all, and we will check to see that you haven't missed a thing. All this ought to take you at least a week" I shot him my most ferocious glare. "And," I growled, "if you give either Jackie or me one more bit of trouble with *anything*, you're going to find yourself instantly in Juvy Hall as an out-of-control kid. If you don't believe me, just try me."

I almost wished he would. I shoved him out of his room, down the stairs and out to our smeared up apartment. I pointed at the hose and a bucket, and told him to get to work.

The boy clearly was stunned at my sudden violent reaction, and immediately started whining that he didn't really mean any harm, and that the paint didn't really do any damage, that he could clean it all up, and on and on. But he did finally clean up his mess. but only by dint of continual badgering by both of us.

A Feud Simmers

Jackie reports. . .

Things around the place finally began to smooth out into a new routine for us with the Langstons gone. Our main work was maintaining and cleaning the enormous house, picking and dead-heading flowers and vegetables. Ed did some touch-up painting around the house, and for me, with a new open account at several exotic local grocery outlets, where money was no object, there was no bargain-hunting for me.

It was almost fun getting used to the new big stove, all the other kitchen gadgets and D'Arcy's amazing collections of exquisite china, crystal, and silverware stored in her spacious pantries. Field supervisor Frank Bartoloman also took time to show both of us George Langston's remarkable collection of antique cars and motorcycles which he kept locked up in that huge fieldstone former winery on the outskirts of the property. We were actually beginning to feel some of our original tension slip away. Then Greg again rocked the boat.

One morning during our usual 7:00 breakfast, someone in a noisy pickup roared into the driveway, rang the back doorbell and banged furiously on the kitchen door. I got up from the table and went to see who was being so outrageously noisy. I opened the door and there stood a huge red-faced, black-haired man wearing a long, thick ponytail, shaking his fist at me through the screen door, yelling, "Where is that little son of a bitch. I'm going to kill him. I. . ."

I interrupted the man with a cold stare and quickly beckoned to Ed to come to the door with me, and snapped, "Who are you, what do you want, and how dare you create such a disturbance here." I was suddenly filled with outrage.

The man calmed a bit saying, "I'm sorry, m'am, but that kid of yours came over to my place in the middle of the night and was fooling around with my thirteen-year-old daugher. I found him in her bedroom this morning, and chased him most of the way over here on foot but lost him on his bike. I came back to our house and got into my truck and that's how I got here. Now where is that little punk?"

It was now about 7:30 on a Saturday, and Greg was, as usual, sleeping in, or so we thought. He rarely wanted much breakfast and we had already learned not to argue with him about it. I finally got around to asking the man's name and where he lived.

"I'm Phil Rizzo, and I work for the Di Rossi winery. We live in that old rambling house down the road from you about a mile. My daughter Abby is in school with your kid Greg and he's been coming over to our place on his bike almost every day. But he'd better not come around again or he'll never make it home."

Ed broke in and introduced both of us, saying, "Mr. Rizzo, Greg is not our son, and his parents are away for a trip out of the country. But, my wife Jackie and I are responsible for him during their absence and we will do all we can to see that he will not bother Abby again. You can be assured we will take care of this problem. We appreciate your letting us know of what he's been up to. Apparently he's been sneaking out of his bedroom after we've gone to bed, and spending his nights who knows where. Believe me, now that you've made us aware of all this, he will be on a much tighter leash."

Rizzo turned away, considerably calmer saying, "Sorry if I upset you people, but I was damned upset myself. Thanks for helping me out." He got into his truck and left a lot more quietly than he had come in.

Now, just what could we do about such sneaky and outrageous behavior? What if he had gotten young Abby pregnant? Should we cable D'Arcy somewhere on a ship in the Mediterannean? We couldn't imprison him in his room, nor could we spend the whole of each day making sure he was staying in school, or all night checking to see if he still was in bed. We decided to consult Frank Bartoloman. He had had a lot of experience in earlier years with this kid. Maybe he had an answer.

We phoned over to Frank in his field office and asked him to come by. He shortly came up to the flagstone patio at the rear of the house, sat down at one of the tables, and put his feet up on a chair. "What can I do for you folks?" he asked.

Ed and I pulled up chairs beside him and over some iced tea we told him about our developing problems with Greg. "Any advice for us with this kid? You've known him a long time and we're baffled. Ed's tempted to haul him down to Juvy Hall as an out-of-control child, but then what? How long would he be in there? Do we really have the right to do such a thing? There are a lot of other things to consider with this boy, too. We've both worked with disturbed children for years, but we also had the resources of the local courts to fall back on where we were well known, as well as the youngsters' families. Here we're operating cold."

I pressed my fingers to my throbbing temples as I thought if only Greg and his parents were coming to us as clients, the problem would be relatively simple. But here we were supposedly hired only as estate managers and were now trying to keep a troubled teenager from destroying his life and perhaps others' as well.

Lean, tanned Frank, his head tilted back with that big stockman's hat hanging on the back of it, thought quietly for a moment, then said, "Well, I have three teen-age boys of my own at home right now, and all of them are pretty feisty. But they have long since learned that when either I or their mother say something, we mean it. They've learned not to try to test us. We really don't have many serious problems with any of them. But Greg here—." He paused and shook his head, "Never has had *any* consistent discipline—*or* affection— from anyone his whole life, and I don't see how you two can make up for what he's been missing for so long.

I nodded in agreement, "But somehow I think we both recognize a tremendous challenge here, and we have to do all we can to deal with Greg's behavior and keep our sanity and our jobs at the same time." Frank assented.

"If I were in your shoes," he said, " I'd tell him that just one more behavior problem and he's headed straight to Juvy Hall. You might also call D'Arcy's attorney and ask his advice. He's been through stuff like this with Greg before at all the prep schools he's been thrown out of. I have his phone number if you want it. But I don't see what other choices you have. Every time D'Arcy and George had problems with him they just shipped him off to a new school, hoping he would somehow straighten out. That hasn't worked, either. Greg has just been a chronic nuisance to them, and when you're rich you get rid of human nuisances by buying them off or sending them away somewhere."

I commented, "It looks to me as if Greg is headed for things a lot more serious than Juvy Hall if he doesn't straighten up and begin to fly right. But I've worked with disturbed kids for years and I can't help but feel that somehow I can reach him with some consistent attention that isn't all negative. I'll bet he hasn't had a compliment or anything positive said to him in his whole life. Sometimes a problem kid will respond if you just praise him for breathing."

We thanked Frank for his help, he headed back to his field office, and we went back into the house for some lunch, and to think over what we might do.

"I want to really try, with a little honest affection, to reach this boy," I said to Ed. "He's really bright, and sometimes very appealing in the few times I've really had a chance to talk with him.. You know, he gets up, dashes off to school and then we don't see him again sometimes till dinner time. I have to try. Let's try a little tough-love."

Tough Love?

Ed reports. . .

Greg, bleary-eyed, finally stumbled into the kitchen for a very late breakfast, clearly not being aware of the fracas we had just had with his young lady love's father.

"Good morning, Greg," Jackie and I chorused. We looked at each other and smiled.

He mumbled a muffled "'morning," and began rummaging through cereal boxes that Jackie had placed on the kitchen table. He found his favorite, Fruit Loops, and poured out a bowl.

I fixed a stare on him and asked, " Well, how'd you sleep last night, Greg."

"Okay, I guess," he said, consciously avoiding my glance.

"Looks to me as if you didn't get very much sleep at all," I said.

He glanced up at me furtively and kept shoveling Fruit Loops into his face, mumbling, "Huh?" as a response.

"Greg, do you know Mr. Rizzo who lives down the road a way from here?"

"Who?" He looked suddenly like a rabbit caught between two hounds.

"Mr. Rizzo. He came by here this morning before you got up, and if you'd seen him you might have wished you were dead," I said, fixing him with another hard stare..

Greg laid down his spoon, wiped his mouth with a napkin, and, radiating panic, suddenly raced out of the room upstairs to his room without saying another word.

Jackie and I looked at each other again as she removed her apron and headed for his room. "Better let me handle this, Ed," she said quietly, and went upstairs.

"Good luck, dear," I muttered.

Jackie reports. . .

On my way up the stairs to Greg's room I kept thinking how much I'd like to wring his neck, but at the same time wanting to hold him close to me, and tell him that Ed and I really are concerned about him and want to help, not just scold him . What could I say or do that would make him believe that people actually cared about him? And would he care?

I knocked on his door, and when he didn't respond I gently pushed it open and found him lying on his rumpled bed with his head buried in a pillow. He was sobbing quietly. I went to the side of his bed and said, "Greg, I know you're hurting. But we must talk." I sat down on the edge of his bed and gently put an arm over him. He allowed my hand to remain as I gently rubbed the tension from his shoulders.

"Greg, do you know how old Abby is?"

He kept his face buried in his pillow, but shook his head.

"Her father told us she's only thirteen. If you had sex with her you could be in very serious trouble on a statutory rape charge. Do you know what that is?"

He suddenly sat up, rubbing his swollen eyes, and blurted,"Rape? I never touched her. She's the only real friend I've ever had. We just talked and talked and hugged and kissed a couple times. Is that so terrible?"

"No, that's not terrible at all," I said. "The big problem here is that you sneaked out of the house here without permission, in the middle of the night, and then apparently spent the rest of the night with her in her bedroom. I think you can see why her father was ready to chop you into little pieces when he found you there."

Greg listened intently to what I was saying, then asked "What's this statuary rape thing you said I could get hit with?"

"The legal term is statutory rape." I spelled it out for him. "It means having sex with an under-age girl, one who is not yet legally able to give her consent for sexual activity. The term statutory means by a statute, or a special law. The penalty for conviction under this law means an almost certain prison term."

Greg, still sobbing a little, shook his head and threw his arms up over his head, saying, "All I wanted to do was talk to her. She's told me she loves me and that her own father doesn't love her and knocks her around. Her mother's dead. We both have the same kind of lousy family relations. Now I'm in trouble just for wanting to talk to someone who cares something about me. No one else ever does." He burst into tears again.

My heart suddenly went out to this troubled boy. It had been clear to us from the moment his mother brought him to stay with us that the two of them were hostile to one another, plus having a step-father who obviously found him a nuisance. Now he was desperately seeking someone, anyone, who would listen to him and bring him something positive in his life, some warmth and affection. I was sure that at his age there was a sex thing there, too, but at this point that didn't seem to be Greg's major problem.

"Greg," I said, "believe me when I say that I really do know and understand exactly the hurt and anger you've been feeling. Both Ed and I have been trained in working with torn up families. Ed has a doctorate in mental health education, and for many years worked with young people who have had problems with their parents. And I've worked with him on many cases, too. Not only that, but we have had seven kids of our own who have had their share of problems. So we do understand the upset you're going through right now, we really do." I leaned closer to him, almost whispering, and said, " I just wanted you to know that we're here to help you, to be your friends, not just ignore you. Nothing is much worse than being ignored by the very people who are really important to us."

Greg, now simmered down, had been been watching me intensely as I talked . "Yeah," he replied, " you can say that again— that bit about being ignored. That's always been the name of the game around here."

I went over to him and gave him a big hug. To my surprise, he hugged back, and said, "Thanks."

"Greg, do you mind telling me what really happened this morning over there at Abby's? You said all you did was talk, right?"

"Yeah, that's right," Greg said. "But we actually were just lying their talking, then were beginning to get kind of hotted up, if you know what I mean,"

I nodded. "Yes, I know what you mean."

"Well, we both had our jeans off and were kind of lying around on the bed just holding each other and talking, when her father suddenly calls up the stairs and asks Abby what she's doing up there. He probably could hear us moving around. 'Nothing,' she yells back, and jumps off the bed reaching for her jeans. I jumped off at the same time and grabbed mine, figuring I'd better get out of there. Then we could hear him coming up the stairs. I almost flipped when I discovered I was trying to get her jeans on and couldn't get them over my hips, and she was flopping around in mine like some kid with her big brother's pants on. Then Abby yelled in kind of a stage whisper, 'Get out the window; I'll handle Dad.' Well, I climbed out the window with her pants half on and half off me, just as the old man opened her door. He saw me and yelled at me that I was a young sonabitch, and he was going to kill me. "I could hear him running back down the stairs as I slid off the roof onto the attached shed and wobbled onto my bike and got back here. You know all the rest. "And," he pleaded, " we really didn't do anything. We really didn't," Greg almost pleaded with me to believe him.

I walked him to his door with one arm around him. "Okay, Greg. I believe you. Now, come on back down to the kitchen. Let's make some waffles together. I have the batter all made."

After his waffles he cheered up a bit and went out to ride his bike, telling us he was just going over to his buddy Hank Rumple's house to work out with his gym set. We knew who the Rumples were and okayed his trip.

I reported to Ed what we had talked about, and told him I felt we had made some real progress.

"Sure hope, so, dear. We're in a pickle if we haven't," he said.

That pickle soon got really sour.

Ed reports. . .

About a week after the Abby Rizzo episode, on a Friday the phone rang at 2:00 a. m., waking us from a deep sleep. Shades of Lingerwood, I thought. Now what. Maybe it was D'Arcy phoning in from Europe. A dozen other possibilities flickered through my fuzzy head as I fumbled for the phone while Jackie reached for a bedside lamp.

"Hello," I mumbled.

A loud male voice on the other end said, "Mr. Langston? This is deputy Williamson. We've got your son down here at sheriff's headquarters. You'd better get down here immediately. He. . ."

Only half awake, I interrupted the caller . "First, I'm not Mr. Langston. My name is Ed Hibler and my wife and I are live-in property managers for the Langstons who are now on a trip out of the country. Now, what's happened with Greg? " I dreaded the answer.

"We caught him, underage, maybe drunk, with no license, with a carfull of other kids and a case of beer in the car. Not only that, he apparently stole the car he was driving. If you have custody of this kid you'd better get down here immediately and get this straightened out. And I'd call your attorney." He hung up abruptly.

I shook my head in disbelief, saying to Jackie, now also fully awake, "Jeez, I don't believe this. After that long talk you had, that kid's in jail for driving with no license, and drunk. And he had a bunch of other kids with him in a car the cops said was stolen. We've got to go down to the Sheriff's office and find out what the hell's been going on. Doesn't look like your tough love was tough enough."

I quickly pulled on a pair of jeans, shoes, tee shirtand a jacket and headed out of our bedroom door, with Jackie scrambling frantically along behind me as she pulled on some clothes.. We rushed down the stairs to our old Datsun and headed into town for the sheriff's office.

We pulled into the sheriff's parking lot, went to the duty officer's desk and identified ourselves. "Are you deputy Williamson?" I asked.

He was a nice looking young man of about thirty-five, with close-cropped hair and rimless glasses, wearing a crisply ironed deputy's uniform. "Right, and you must be the Hiblers. I'm sorry we had to shake you out of bed, but this kid's been a chronic problem in these parts for years. I thought he was away in school somewhere."

"He has been, but just came home before the Langstons took off on a trip to the Mediterranean. We've been told that he's been expelled from several schools. We haven't been on this job ourselves for more than a couple of months," I explained. "Now what's happened here with Greg?"

"Well, as I told you on the phone, he was picked up earlier this evening with three other boys, all underage, by one of our patrol officers. I'm told by the arresting officer that he failed a sobriety test, and had no driver's license. And we found several opened cans of beer in the car plus another half case unopened. Not only that, the car he was driving he apparently stole. He refuses to tell us where he picked it up and we haven't yet checked out the license plates which seem to be collector's plates. The car is an old Studebaker Avanti. . ." Bingo! One of George Langston's antique cars! I had owned one myself thirty or more years ago when they were considered a dramatic change in Studebaker's sturdy but increasingly stodgy image.

"May we see Greg?" I asked Williamson

"Sure, I'll go bring him out." He left his desk and went back down a long corridor. In a couple of minutes he appeared with Greg, head downcast, stumbling along in front of him. They came to a bench at the side of the room and we all sat down.

"Officer," I said, "May we talk with Greg privately for a few moments?" Williamson nodded, then went to his desk to answer a phone call.

Greg sat, head downcast, noticeably trembling. "Greg, do you want to tell us what happened tonight?" I tried not to sound too authoritarian. Greg just shook his head and kept his head down.

Jackie then asked, "Greg, I thought we had a deal. If you had some problems, you could tak with me or Ed any time and we'd work it out together. Have I let you down somehow?" He shook his head again, but finally looked up at us, eyes brimming.

"All I wanted to do was have some fun with Hank and a couple of his friends," he sobbed. "We thought we could take one of George's cars out for a little spin around the neighborhood. Then Hank opened some beer he'd brought and before we knew it this cop came up to where we were parked and shined his flashlight in our eyes and ordered us to get out. Then he made us bend over the hood of the car, and frisked us, and then called in for help. They said I was drunk and I wasn't. Then they brought us all down here and called our parents." He burst fully into deep, heavy weeping, repeating over and over again, "I'm a loser, a born loser. I can't do anything right. Now Abby'll hate me, too"

The parents of the other boys involved apparently had already retrieved their culprits, leaving just Greg for us. Williamson watched us from his desk as he answered phone calls. It was now nearly four o'clock in the morning, and I went over to his desk and asked if Greg could be released into our custody. I would get the phone number of Langston's attorney from Frank in the morning and call him for advice.

We signed some release papers, as Williamson noted that he would keep George's classic Studebaker impounded until the case against Greg and his buddies was heard or settled. I asked him if he thought Greg should be sent to Juvenile Hall.

"I suggest you discuss what happened with Mr. Hastings, Langston's attorney in the morning, and he can take it from there," he said. "Good luck. Looks as if you're going to need it." The three of us walked slowly out to the car just as dawn was beginning to break over the nearby mountains.

On the way home we asked Greg how he had been able to get the Studebaker out of his step-dad's winery-garage. "That was easy," he said, "I kept my bike in there and had a key to the door padlock. George always left the keys to all those cars and motocycles in a desk drawer in the old winery. I knew where they were and figured we could have the car back before anyone even found out it was missing."

"Greg," I said, glaring at him, " you're now in real trouble. You've been charged with being an under-age, unlicensed driver, driving a motor vehicle while under the influence, and grand theft auto. There may be other charges, too. It's enough to put you away for a long time without expert legal help. First thing in the morning we will go into town and talk with your mother's attorney. You're going to need his services if there's any chance of keeping you out of Juvenile Hall or, worse, the California Youth Authority. That's a prison for habitual under-age criminals. " Greg just kept his head down, saying nothing.

As we drove into the driveway and up to the back of the house, I closed our encounter, saying, "Now get up to bed and try to get some sleep. And if you leave your room again without our permission I'll have you back at the Sheriff's office before you know what hit you."

He dragged himself up the stairs to his room as Jackie and I exchanged worried shrugs.

"Now, what's next?" Jackie asked as we fell into bed ourselves.

Jackie reports. . .

My compassion for this bad-attitude kid was rapidly dwindling away. We expected these years to be enjoying our own grandchildren, not agonizing over the antics of a troubled teenager who had been dumped in our lap.

We were both exhausted from being up most of the night, and now some difficult decisons had to be made. I made a pot of strong black tea, though neither one of us had an appetite for breakfast.

I looked up the number that our employers had left in the event of emergencies. It was interesting to note that the name of the vet for the animals came first, then the family doctor and dentist and, finally, the name of the lawyer we were looking for, a Mr. Stephen Hastings. Darn, he was in San Francisco, more than two hours away. I guessed the Langstons figured that in a small community where they were located it would be too risky to use an attorney in such a limited area. Any negative stories could get around too quickly.

I washed our cups, fed the whining animals, then went up-stairs to check on Greg. He had fallen asleep with the look of an angelic but frowning child on his face. I closed his door softly and went back to the kitchen to begin my daily routine.

We kept a close rein on Greg over the rest of that week-end, and I put a call in to Hastings at 8:00a. m. on Monday, stressing to his secretary that this was extremely urgent business. I told her I would expect a return call within the hour.

Hastings returned my call with unexpected promptness and I quickly filled him in on our problem with Greg. He said, "Can you come in tomorrow at 9:00?" I agreed, and we now had our prophetic date.

Hasting's office was on the top floor of one of San Francisco's tallest buildings, with views of the entire Bay area. We were seated promptly by one of the firm's secretaries, and were told that Hastings would be with us shortly.

In a few minutes he opened his office door, beckoned the three of us to come in, then closed the door behind us. He was tall, graying, wore steel-rimmed glasses, and walked with a slight stoop. After mutual introductions he said, "Please sit down. Would you like some coffee? He held a thermos decanter in one hand. We politely demurred, and after taking a swallow or two from his own cup, Hastings spoke directly to Greg.

"Greg, we've had talks before. Remember?" Greg, head down, nodded. "But this time you're going to have to appear in court to face very serious charges. This isn't just raising hell at your school any more. Would you like to tell me how in the devil you ever got yourself into this dumb fix?"

Greg shifted around in his chair, obviously stressed out, and in a low mumbling voice recounted the events of the previous week-end. His story was about what he had already told us, as Hastings jotted notes. In a few minutes, he leaned back in his big leather chair, buzzed his secretary outside the office, and asked her to take Greg into an adjoining office while he talked with us. Greg left, looking over his shoulder at us. Panic was now clearly in his eyes.

Hastings now turned to us as we sat directly across from his desk.

"We have a tricky problem here," he said. "Neither of you are legal guardians of this kid, whether or not his parents told you so when they left him with you. You have no legal way of enforcing any discipline, or even getting him medical care in their absence. I'm afraid this has been typical of the way the Langston's have handled Greg since he was little—just pawn him off on someone else if he got in the way of their own plans." He turned to his phone and asked his secretary to put in a call for a Mr. Fenway.

"I think I might have a solution to this for you," he said to us, covering the phone with his hand as it rang.. "Would you mind waiting in the front office while I take this call? We'll get together again after I'm through." His party answered as we momentarily left and sat near his secretary in his outer office.

Hastings was on the phone for a lengthy time, but when he finally had finished his conversation, he called us back into his office.

"I have just had a long talk with Harold Fenway. Does that name mean anything to you?" We both shook our heads. "Well, Mr. Fenway is an old friend of mine and just happens to be D'Arcy Langston's step-brother. They have never liked one another over the years, but for some reason he's had a warm spot in his heart for young Greg. He used to have him over at his ranch near Mendocino on the coast quite often during summers when Greg was little, while D'Arcy and one of her current husbands took one of their long cruises or trips around the world. He and Greg became quite close during those years. He has never had any children of his own, and he is now widowed. I told him about Greg's new problem, and because it is now near the end of the school year, he said, 'Send him over here to me. We'll do fine.' Does that sound encouraging."

I looked at Ed, and he at me, relief flooding over us both. "Boy, does it!" Ed exclaimed.

Hastings continued, "Hal Fenway and I have been friends for years, and I had planned to run over his way this coming weekend anyway, just to get away for a few hours. Now then, you have Greg, with his needed clothes and things here at my office Friday afternoon at five o'clock. I'll meet you in the parking garage here in the building. Meantime, I'll take care of his problem with the sheriff—I know him, too—and will handle D'Arcy when she returns. She hates negative publicity, and I'm sure she will do what I suggest with Greg."

He then called the boy back into the office with the rest of us. "Greg," he said with one arm around the boy's shoulder, "You and I are going to take a trip over to see your Uncle Hal this Friday. In the meantime I'll work with your sheriff's department on your problem with them. Dr. and Mrs. Hibler are working with me on all of this, and, in the meantime, you will be totally under their control till I see you Friday afternoon. Bring whatever you need for an extended visit with your uncle."

Greg looked absolutely flabbergasted. "You mean I'm not going to have to go to court, or jail or anything?"

"'I can't guarantee anything, Greg, but I think we can work things out, both with the sheriff's office and your mother when she gets back. In the meantime you'd better toe the mark with the Hiblers, or you may suddenly find yourself locked up.."

His phone rang, we shook hands quickly, and went back to the car for the drive back to the Langston's mansion. None of us had much to say during the two-hour trip, but it was with immense relief that we drove into the Langston's place that evening and tumbled into bed.

That Homecoming Bash

Ed reports. . .

The rest of that week rolled by with no further problems with Greg. In fact he was almost cheeerful and even offered to help

Jackie around the house. On Thursday we spent much of the day gathering up his needed clothes and personal effects for his trip to his uncle's place, and I specifically made sure that his paint-ball stuff was not included. He seemed happy, even eager, to get going, and Friday morning, after an early breakfast, the three of us left left for San Francisco and our rendezvous with Hastings.

As arranged, we met him in his office building's garage, where we transferred Greg's stuff to his big Buick wagon. We had some hearty goodbyes, thanked Hastings for all his help, and Jackie and I each gave Greg big hugs. Surprisingly, he hugged us back, and actually said he was sorry for giving us all such a bad time.

Jackie said, "Greg, we'd love to stay in touch with you. Please let us know how you're doing, and what your plans will be for this fall and school. Oh, and we'll keep your problems with us our special secret, okay?" He nodded and waved a goodbye as we drove out of the parking garage and into the sunlit street.

Back at the house we were greeted with a cablegram from D'Arcy, telling us she and George would be back in San Francisco the following week. They would be out to our place on that week-end. Both Jackie and I greeted the news with mixed feelings. It was great that our problem with Greg was apparently solved, but now we were facing our first real experiences in dealing directly with D'Arcy and George.

They arrived as expected, and called from their San Franicsco home. Jackie answered the phone, welcomed them home, and told D'Arcy that Greg had gone over to her step-brother's place in Mendocino for a visit, and that otherwise everything was fine. D'Arcy told us that she and George were planning a coming-home party for the following Saturday, and that she was calling caterers to have her party all ready to go by the time they were to arrive. She said we could expect about fifty friends to be there. She had asked absolutely nothing about Greg.

Just how she would manage to advise so many people of the party on such short notice was a mystery, but she apparently had been doing things like this for years. With enough money miracles are easy.

That ensuing week we worked frantically to be sure that everything in the huge house and the immediate gardens around it were in good shape for their arrival. In the meantime, we had had a talk with Frank Bartoloman and told him about our resolution of the Greg problem, and he agreed that we had lucked out with Hastings. He also gave us a few tips on how to get ready for the coming week-end's party, saying that D'Arcy would almost certainly have invited some of her newspaper columnist buddies and several others bigwigs reported often in the City's society pages.

On Thursday morning D'Arcy called to say they were on their way. Joan earlier had told Jackie that D'Arcy always wanted fresh cut flowers in every room every day, and we had gathered dozens of bouquets from the vast gardens surrounding the house. Every bedroom and all of the sprawling lounge areas downstairs were now filled with fresh flowers.

In due time we met them as they drove George's red Ferrari into the garage shortly after noon. After their somewhat perfunctory greetings, I helped carry their luggage into the house. I breezily asked how their trip had gone. D'Arcy ignored my question and George tossed out an "Okay" over one shoulder as he headed for his bathroom.

Neither of them asked about Greg, nor did D'Arcy have any comment whatever about the appearance of the house and all of the flowers we had cut and arranged for her. Apparently it was something she routinely expected and hence deserved no comment. We were soon to discover just how totally ego-centered these two would prove to be.

Jackie had by now enough practice with the elaborate kitchen equipment to feel quite confident that she could handle whatever cooking needed to be done, especially when it was almost always only on an occasional week-end. And this party was being catered and hence would require only our help with serving guests and being sure their drinks and hors d'oeuvres were promptly refreshed.

D'Arcy called the two of us into the kitchen on Friday evening, and explained how their catered affairs usually were programmed. The caterers would appear in the morning bringing all required equipment, food, and other party accouterments, and would set up their tables on the extensive flagstone terraces ringing the house and the pool. Their staff would include two bartenders and two waiters who would also double as bus-boys and help clear up the tables after the dinner.

A small jazz combo would set up alongside the pool, and a satellite bar would be set up in the large poolhouse, really a snug guest house, which adjoined the pool. Our assignments were to circulate among the guests, making sure that everyone was properly served with drinks and hors o'oeuvres. We were relieved that we were not required to wear either a butler's or waitress's uniform, but being casually dressed, could mingle unobtrusively among the guests, helping whenever it seemed appropriate.

I kept getting deja vu visions of Sin-Bed's eleborate and diastrous lawn party, but saw no evidence here of any problems with bees or other calamitous wildlife. Guests began arriving around three o'clock the next day, and by four o'clock the entire large parking area around the big garage had been filled with a variety of luxury cars. I noted two Bentley's, three Rolls-Royces, a couple of BMW's, half a dozen Mercedes, and three chauffeur-driven Cadillac stretch limousines. I had a brief flash of uneasiness as I remembered my driving Lulu's stretch limo and the weird experiences we had during our brief but miserable time with them.

As the sun went down and dusk gathered, the whole terrace and pool area took on an almost Disneyland atmosphere. Hundreds of tiny twinking lights winked from the many trees and shrubs surrounding the scene. Floating candles glided among magnolia blossoms on the swimming pool. Jackie giggled at the thought of movie queen Esther Williams popping up through the blossoms and candles. Yet who in this crowd would even know who she was?

The jazz combo, imported by D'Arcy from a favorite City

watering hole, played lots of nostalgic show tunes from Hoagy Carmichel to Cole Porter. Clouds of aromatic steam wafted from bubbling chafing dishes, as society babble and laughter swept the convivial gathering. As we circulated we noted and spoke briefly with a number of well-known City columnists, one faux European count, and several people from the Los Angeles movie colony. We actually were surprised at the general good cheer of the event, and at the real lack of any loutish drunkenness which we had anticipated after some of the Frank Bartoloman stories of earlier parties. Both D'Arcy and George played the affable hosts to the hilt, and though George was well tiddly by the time guests were beginning to filter back out to their cars, he generally behaved himself with good cheer. Until later that night.

The party had pretty well petered out by two a. m., all the guests had said their well-wishes to their hosts, and Jackie and I now made our way up to our garage apartment which overlooked part of the pool and terraced areas of the party. But first I made sure all the lights were out and doors were secure. The caterers would be back in the morning for a clean-up.

Neither Jackie nor I were used to such late hours, and we really crashed into bed that night. Then, at about three-thirty, shouting and yelling awakened us. It was coming from out by the pool. Both of us clambered out of bed in the dark, blinking groggily as we peered through the curtains to see who was making all the racket. It was D'Arcy and George. He was unsteadily waving a highball glass in one hand while he thrashed a golf club through the air with the other, apparently aiming it at D'Arcy, who easily side-stepped every swish. It was an unbelievable sight.

Bellowing drunkenly at her, he was accusing her of making out with two of the younger men at the party. "Goddamn whore," he roared, lost his balance and fell into the pool. D'Arcy now burst into hysterical laughter, screeching, "You drunken bastard! I hope you drown." She staggered uncertainly back towards the terrace around the house. "That'll cool you off, you aging jerk," she screamed as she disappeared right under our window into the kitchen. George, still slashing his golf club around in the pool, finally crawled up the pool steps at the shallow end, fell onto one of the poolside chaises, and passed out. He remained there, like a besotted beached whale, the rest of the night.

Jackie and I clambered back into bed, wondering if this was going to be a pattern with these two out-of-control millionaires for the rest of our stay with them. We didn't have long to find out.

The next morning D'Arcy slept in till nearly noon, while George, still reeking with booze, finally stumbled into the kitchen from the pool area, looking like he'd been ten rounds with Mohammed Ali. He totally ignored both of us and fumbled his way up the back stairs to their bedroom.

We never let either D'Arcy or George know what we had seen that wild night, and for the next couple of weeks or so things went routinely with both of them back in their City home.

Jackie reports. . .

One morning shortly thereafter we got a call from D'Arcy saying George would be out of town for an extended period, and that she was coming out by herself for a brief stay. She would have several of her tennis buddies in for breakfast later, she said.

She arrived as scheduled, driving her own gold Rolls Royce Corniche convertible into the garage. She walked briskly through the kitchen with an airy hello and wave of a hand and immediately settled down by the phone at the end of the room. For the next three hours she talked almost continuously both to the society editor of one of The City's daily papers, and to a variety of her friends, regaling them all with tales of her recent trip. She invited several of them for a breakfast-brunch the following day, and gave me instructions about what she wanted served, and that they would meet and eat on the terrace by the pool.

The following morning her lady friends began arriving about ten o'clock. Six of them greeted one another with excited shrieks, hugs and girlish chatter as they gathered around tables Ed had set up near the pool. From my position in the kitchen, and while running back and forth with their breakfast I got an earful of the lifestyle of the super-rich and not so famous, though several of the women were, indeed, well known either as writers or as fixtures in Bay Area society circles. I especially found Lola Lanterman a fascinating study.

Lola is a widely known fiftyish novelist who grinds out new romantic bosom-heaving best selling pot-boilers almost weekly. Mother of four children, tall, bleached-blonde, and always tanned, she has been married to several different men of substance during her literary pursuits, including an internationally known editor and publisher, a world-class producer of fine portraiture and sculpture, and one big game hunter known for his collections of costly taxidermy and elegant women. Between marriages—and sometimes during—she also was reported to have had numerous affairs with others of her glitzy tomcat society.

Listening to her babble on about some of her recent steamy peccadillos was better than watching soaps on TV. The other women, all at that stage in their lives where plastic surgery was taking over from diets and couture, listened wide-eyed to Lola's tales as she reminisced, orgasm to orgasm. Currently single, she made fun of most of her current conquests, hysterically describing most of them in typically salty rhetoric as either dithering pricks or withering pricks, depending on their ages. Her listeners broke into screaming fits of laughter after each tale.

I was tempted to stay as close to the gathering as I could, but duty kept me moving back and forth to the kitchen. But I gathered enough gossip from this one morning's crop to keep any reader of supermarket tabloids dizzy for a month. But it was an event that happened the following week-end that had us both flabbergasted.

Reluctant Voyeurs

Ed reports. . .

Jackie and I fortunately got time off without loss of income whenever D'Arcy or George were not planning to be "on campus." This particular week-end we had planned to take our venerable old motor home up to a campground near Lake Tahoe, about a three-hour trip. We asked D'Arcy if we could have the time off and she agreed, saying she would be in The City during that time.

On Sunday we loaded up and headed out of town for a needed change of scenery. Then, less than a mile out of town, we had engine trouble. The old bucket began to miss and snort, much as she had when we were stalled in that terrible heat en route to Lulu's place. I looked at Jackie, she at me, and we both agreed we'd better get back to Langstonville while she was still running, and try the trip later. We stumbled back through the gates of the estate and parked the motor home behind George's old winery building well out of sight of the house. Our little Datsun remained parked in its usual stall in the carport next to the garage.

We kind of fell back into our usual routines and in the evening, after taking a long walk around the beautiful grounds, we decided to watch a bit of TV and hit the hay early. I wanted to get the gimpy motor home over to a local mechanic the moment he opened his shop the next morning.

We were awakened after we had barely gone to sleep with the sound of a car driving up and into the garage right under our windows. We listened for voices, but heard nothing but the slamming of a car door, and the rumble of a garage door coming down on the space where D'Arcy always parked her Rolls. She was back, but just what brought her this time wasn't clear. We dropped off to sleep again only to be reawakened at about midnight with soft laughter and the murmuring of voices down by the pool. We could hear D'Arcy laughing and a man's voice chuckling along with her. There was something oddly familiar about that male voice. Both

Jackie and I looked at one another in the gloom of the bedroom and both got out of bed, leaving the lights off, to see what was going on out there.

The underwater pool lights gave the whole area a soft almost ethereal glow, but now we could make out who was down there with D'Arcy. It was Frank Bartoloman.

Fascinated, we watched an amazing tableau develop poolside. Both D'Arcy and Frank wore swimming togs, she a skimpy bikini, he brief shorts—very brief. Laughing, D'Arcy slowly walked toward Frank, provocatively swaying her hips. She threw her arms around his neck and planted a passionate open- mouth kiss on him as she leaped upwards and wrapped both long legs around his waist. He pulled her close against him as both, off balance now, fell into the pool. Shrieking with laughter, D'Arcy chased Frank up the steps at the shallow end of the pool where the two of them crashed onto an oversize chaise. In seconds she had pulled Frank's shorts to below his knees, and her bikini also somehow disappeared under the chaise.

Jackie whispered, "I really don't think we should be watching this, do you?"

"Well, we *are* watching it, aren't we?" I hissed back at her. "I find it all fascinating. Go back to bed if you want to. I'm not going to miss this show."

"Well, if you're going to watch, then I have to too," Jackie said.

Obviously, we watched.

The next five minutes or so were a wild shrieking, moaning, and gasping orgy of out of control poolside passion. They rolled off the chaise onto pads and towels on the pool deck, and after several more minutes of thrashing and humping around together, they separated, gasping for breath, and laughing together.

"God! What a roll," Frank exclaimed. All D'Arcy could do was nod, gasp and smile as she reached out for him again and pulled him on top of her once more.

Jackie and I remained frozen at our window until both of them finally got up, gathered towels and, giggling softly to each other, walked unsteadily towards the kitchen door with their arms around each other. We heard the kitchen door slam shut and saw the light from its window go out. Apparently they were planning to spend the rest of the night together.

We looked at one another, shook our heads, hardly believing what we had just witnessed. Jackie said, "Wow!" I said, "Jeez!" and we crawled back into bed.

The next morning before I could get up to get the motor home over to the mechanic, I heard D'Arcy's garage door roll up and her Rolls back out into the driveway. Then I heard Frank's pickup start up farther down the driveway. They were both apparently en route "home."

At breakfast Jackie and I discussed the amazing scene of the night before and wondered just what had been going on with D'Arcy and Frank. Frank was married with teen-age kids, and we had met his very lovely wife several times as she visited the place during his working hours. D'Arcy apparently was just simply following the general behavioral pattern of her social group. George was out of town; Frank was available. It was that simple. I couldn't help but wonder if D'Arcy was going to report this orgiastic experience to her girl friends at their next joint breakfast.

The place remained quiet and peaceful for the next week or so. Frank came over one day at lunch time to see how we were doing, but there wasn't a hint that anything unusual had gone on in his life recently. We chatted a bit about doings around the estate, he gave us a cheery wave, and drove his pickup back to his office across the property.

Then, out of the blue came a phone call from Bob and Joan Renney. They were back from their extended Italian vacation trip and had already found themselves another job doing much the same thing for another wealthy family, this time in Contra Costa County, north of Vallejo. They wanted to know how we had been doing with D'Arcy and George. We made a date to see them on the following week-end to get caught up on what had been going on with both of us.

We met them for lunch in a favorite restaurant near St. Helena where we had met several times over a year before. They excitedly told us all about their nearly a month in northern Italy and showed us snapshots from their trip. They also said that their new employers, much like D'Arcy and George, were away from their big place most of the time, leaving them to do mainly simple caretaking chores. They said they would probably spend another year at this kind of work and then would take their savings, now tens of thousands of dollars, and invest them in their own catering business. Everything they had planned was now coming to a successful close.

We then brought them up to date on our jobs with D'Arcy and George, the fiasco with young Greg, and the amazing erotica we had witnessed by the pool between D'Arcy and Frank.

"I had always suspected that those two had something going," said Joan. "I had watched them together on a number of occasions. D'Arcy is a compulsive flirt anyway, but I felt that she had something going with him a long time ago."

Bob nodded in agreement.

Jackie said, "We've just been wondering whether or not we should try and stay in this job. It certainly pays us well for what we do, but both Ed and I feel very uneasy around this kind of lifestyle and wonder if we could find something else without all the wild libido. Also, we have had virtually no positive feedback from either D'Arcy or George on how we're doing."

Joan said, "Don't expect any. You'll know you're doing okay when they never comment on anything. It's when things happen that they don't like, then you'll hear about it. Seems to me you've been doing fine."

"Well, I hope you're right," Jackie replied. "I just have this continuous uneasy feeling when they're around. Thank heavens it's usually only on week-ends."

We finished lunch, said goodbyes and promised to stay in closer touch.

Joan said, as she got in their car, "You know, Jackie, how we have always liked to check out newspaper ads for estate managing help just to see what's going on in our line of work? Well, if we see anything you might be interested in we'll buzz you." And off they went.

It was great seeing the two of them again, and we felt a bit of a recharge as we went back to Langston's lair. But now D'Arcy was planning a dinner party for a dozen or so guests the coming weekend which meant we had to get down to work, Jackie in the grocery department and kitchen, and me around the house and gardens, neatening up the whole area, and collecting and arranging the usual house fresh flower displays once again. This would be really our first dinner assignment, and both of us were a bit apprehensive. I also suddenly realized that I needed to bone up on my neglected butlering duties.

Gaffes in Spades

It was nearly dark as the guests arrived. One couple drove in with a new BMW sedan followed by two others in Caddies and Lincolns. Another arrived in a little Mazda sports coupe; six couples altogether, all of them were dressed for a semi-formal dinner. The men wore either jackets with turtleneck sweaters and slacks, or suits. The ladies all arrived in fur coats or jackets—it was beginning to get chilly outside— with either smart tailored suits or elegant designer dresses underneath. Dressed in my formal white butler's jacket with brass buttons, I met them all at the front door, taking their coats and hats, and tried to be affable but discreet as I welcomed them and directed them into the big lounge for cocktails and hors d'oevres.

Jackie in the kitchen was busy filling puff shells with lobster and stuffing large mushroom caps with an herb dressing mixture. She had already prepared a tray of caviar and cucumber hors d'oevres and other tasty goodies for me to distribute as they quaffed their cocktails. George acted as his own bartender and was in his affable party self as I picked up and distributed his trays of drinks and nibbles.

As usual, the men gathered at one end of the huge room at the bar talking politics, sports or business, while the women gabbed away with their own interests at the other. I noted that none of these women were among D'Arcy's breakfast buddies, but that one was a society columnist for one of The City's papers. I recognized one of the men as the president of a large City exporting company. He had been at Sin-Bed's disastrous lawn party earlier that year. Another was a widely known sportscaster and writer, and standing next to him, talking about something with great enthusiasm, was San Francisco's beloved Herb Caen, nationally known columnist and venerable commentator on the foibles of Baghdad by the Bay, as he had in his column long ago affectionately dubbed his beloved city.

Within a half hour Jackie notified D'Arcy that dinner was ready and I formally announced it. D'Arcy led the elegant group to the dining room where the men seated their ladies. I returned to the kitchen to check on things with Jackie who had been working furiously to get the evening's fine meal ready. We were having herb-laced jellied consomme followed by beef medallions that Jackie had marinated in pomegranate juice, to be served with a roasted garlic sauce and fresh vegetables directly from our gardens, as the main entre. For those guests who were not eating red meat we had mesquite-grilled chicken scented with coriander. With this we presented Roma tomatoes stuffed with baby green limas seasoned with a light garlic sauce, and served with a chicken-broth-and-butter-seasoned rice pilaf. Also on the table were a variety of breads and rolls. Dessert would be either a melon sorbet with lime, made right in our own kitchen with that $1,200 machine, or chocolate ice cream with a black muscat sauce. A variety of liqueurs and/ or a demi-tasse of coffee would conclude the meal.

Earlier we had discovered that almost everything in the kitchen had some kind of a bell or buzzer attached to it. The two dishwashers buzzed when they went into their drying cycle, the sorbet machine ding-dinged when it was through, the commercial toaster had a gong-like sound when it popped up, and then there was D'Arcy's damned little table bell.

My job as butler was to be specially attentive to the needs of guests without being obtrusive, and whenever D'Arcy rang her little table bell I was to appear to take away or retrieve whatever she needed.

They had finished the consomme course and I had removed all those dishes, remembering from my experiences with Lulu that "you serve from the left and remove from the right." Things were coming along swimmingly when I again heard that table bell ding and immediately walked from the kitchen into the dining room abuzz with loud table conversation. D'Arcy turned over her shoulder to me and asked me to get her a fly swatter. I thought it an odd request, especially at a formal dinner table. But when I brought it to her she snapped, "What's this for? Why would you bring me this nasty thing?

I was totally confused. "I asked you for ice water, you dummy!" She glared at me as I quickly retreated to the kitchen with the fly swatter. Fly swatter and ice water. I knew my hearing was going, but this was acutely embarrassing, especially with the laughter of her guests echoing into the kitchen.

But this was only the beginning of what became a memorable evening.

I was serving the main entree, the medallions of beef, with a lively conversation going on between one of the women and a man across the table. They were arguing about how to diagnose a mutual friend who had become mentally ill. He apparently had "lost it," as she put it, and was hearing voices and seeing things that weren't there. He had been picked up and committed to a local mental health facility for observation. She said he was psychotic, but he insisted that the proper term for his condition was psychopathic.

As a retired psychologist and therapist I simply couldn't resist clarifying their little difference, and as I served the lady her entree,

I spoke to her and said, "Madame, I hope you will forgive me, but as a retired psychology professor and therapist perhaps I can clarify a difference for you both here. Someone who is hallucinating like your friend, and hears voices or sees things that do not exist, is clearly psychotic, meaning that his 'psyche' or mental state is out of touch with reality in some way. The term 'psychopathic' refers to behavior of someone who is clearly in touch with reality, but who is acting in ways that are 'pathological' or 'sick' in his ability to socialize normally with others. Our prisons are full of these people. . ."

"Ed-WARD!" It was D'Arcy glaring at me as her guests had been riveted with what I had been saying to the arguing couple. "You are needed in the kitchen!" She waved her hand and pointed to the door.

Only then did I realize that I had quite absent-mindedly committed one of the worst gaffes any butler can perpetrate—mixing into the conversations with guests. I offered my apologies to the group and quickly retreated into the kitchen where I told Jackie what I had done. She put her hand over her mouth, saying "Oh, you didn't, you didn't! Oh, no, we're dead here. I warned you about mixing in with guests. You blew it. What next!"

The rest of the dinner and evening went fairly smoothly, though I felt that every time I reentered the dining room that D'Arcy was burning holes through my back with her eyes.

The next morning as we were cleaning up the remaining debris from the party D'Arcy floated into the kitchen uncharacteristically wearing a housecoat, but with her makeup and hair impeccably applied. It was only nine o'clock and she usually didn't appear, especially after a party, until ten or later.

She came right to the point and asked us to come in to the dining room to the table where we all sat down together.

"Ed," she began in her deep-throated whiskey voice, "what you did last night at this table was appalling. With your education you certainly should have known that a *servant*-"-here she emphasized the word —"never becomes involved in the conversations with guests unless he is asked to. What you did was humiliating for me and George and a reflection on my good judgment in hiring you."

Jackie sat beside me listening intently and watching every twitch in her heavily mascaraed eyes.

I stared back directly at D'Arcy and said, simply, "You are absolutely right, Mrs. Langston. It was a terrible gaffe, and I sincerely apologize for it. I guess I felt that I might be of help to the two people who were having a friendly argument about something with which I have had a great deal of experience. I goofed, and I'm sorry."

There was a brief silence. Then Jackie spoke up, looking intently at D'Arcy. "Mrs. Langston, you may remember that when Ed and I first talked with you before Joan and Bob left, you said you needed no further references or background checks on us because of their strong recommendations of us for this job.

"Also, at that meeting you never told us that Greg would be coming here for us to care for and supervise, and we now know that at that time you were quite aware of his coming, despite your later denial. You left in our care, without our accepting the task, a totally undisciplined boy with a history of bad behavior in school and elsewhere, without any notice or apparent concern for our capacity—or desire—to take care of him . In addition to that experience, while we have generally found working for you interesting and satisfactory, we have at the same time witnessed and heard a number of things here that lead us to believe that we probably are not the right people for you."

Jackie then looked directly at me, eyebrows raised, as if asking if what she had said was right. I nodded, saying, "Yes, I agree with Jackie. I think we may have made a serious mistake in coming here. It was Bob and Joan who were so sure that we would be right for you. We apparently don't have the right chemistry or backgrounds to fulfill what you need done here."

D'Arcy seemed momentarily stunned at our reaction, apparently expecting we would bow our heads meekly and abjectly curtsy our way back into the kitchen. She got up from the table abruptly, turned, saying absolutely nothing, and went back upstairs, leaving Jackie and me to stare at one another and shrug.

Jackie later told me that the thought had flashed through her mind that it might be fun to mention to D'Arcy that we had inadvertently witnessed her midnight romp with Frank, but thought better of it. Could we have maybe doubled our salaries with a bit of discreet blackmail? No, we just didn't play the game that way. "Well, now where do we go?" Jackie asked of no one in particular. Incredibly, less than an hour later, we had a possible answer with a phone call from Bob and Joan. As they had promised, they had seen several help-wanted ads for domestic help that they had checked out, and thought we might be interested in following up on some of them.

We told them of my gaffe at dinner the previous night—which they thought was hysterically funny—and of our brief, blunt talk with D'Arcy. We jotted down the three phone numbers and pertinent data about each job that they had picked out of the paper and thanked them, telling them we would report in as soon as we had checked them out.

We had now been at the Langston's place about eight months, and while our income was dramatically better than it had been with Ahmed and Ada Longstreet, and we had indeed been able to save substantial money by living in with most of our personal expenses covered, we still felt we had a long way to go before we could consider ourselves even near the edge of the financial woods. Much of our earned income was being used to simply keep up payments on our unsold house. It still had not been sold, though the real estate market had slowly improved. Hence, though we periodically became depressed and homesick, we knew we had to keep plugging somewhere for probably at least another year.

Following up once more on Joan and Bob's newspaper referrals seemed the sensible way to go before we gave D'Arcy any formal notice.

CHAPTER 6

Goats, Goats, Goats and
Living it Up With the Branburys

Jackie reports. . .

I methodically made calls to each of Bob and Joan's referrals, only to discover that one of the three positions advertised had already been filled. But the second one sounded interesting. The woman answering the phone identified herself as Megan Branbury, owner with her consort Marlon, of a large suburban estate in Sonoma County, actually scarcely thirty miles from the Langstons' place. She said that she had recently lost the services of a couple who had been with her for a number of years, and now was searching for a compatible replacement.

I gave her a brief description of ourselves, our work history, where we were working now, and why as professional people we had chosen this way to augment our quite inadequate retirement income. I told her we were both in certifiable excellent health and anxious to make a change in our work situation as soon as possible, mentioning D'Arcy' and George's name. In response I thought I heard a subdued chuckle.

"So you've been working for D'Arcy, have you?" she commented. "I think I can see why you might be seeking other employment." Apparently the Langston's reputation had gotten around.

I made a date with her for us to meet her and her husband on Sunday of the following week-end when we were off duty. However, before we saw her I called the remaining ad also, and made an appointment to meet with that party on the preceding Saturday. The owner wasn't home, but a caretaker answering my call made a date for us to meet with the owners, a couple named Terracline. This place was clear on the opposite side of the Sonoma area, apparently almost into the hilly country around Lake Berryessa. So, now we had two interviews scheduled for the next week-end, one with the Terraclines on Saturday, the Branburys on Sunday.

D'Arcy had returned to their City home right after our blunt confrontation, and we didn't expect to see much more of her again until George returned from his trip, probably at least two more weeks. We settled into our usual routines until Saturday morning, when we arose early, had a quick breakfast and headed over to the Terraclines' home in warm early autumn sunshine.

It was at least an hour's drive from D'Arcy's place to this first interview. We wandered at first through the eastern part of the Napa Valley, then up into hilly brush-covered country studded with bull pine, lots of manzanita, and large oaks. We finally found the Terracline's home situated atop a large oak-studded hill with views to the west of Lake Berryessa and surrounding vineyards. The split-level house was a very impressive French provincial style, built of soft-colored fieldstone and old brick, with a slate roof and large French windows in rows across two sides of of the building. Several chimneys thrust through the heavy slate, indicating multiple fireplaces in the interior.

We parked the car in the back-out area of a four-car garage, walked around the end of the house to a beautifully crafted stained-glass front door, and rang the bell.

A bosomy, very attractive fortyish blonde with an upswept hairdo, dressed in tight-fitting jeans and open-necked white blouse, answered the door with a big smile and introduced herself as Blanche Terracline.

"You must be the Hiblers," she gushed. "Our caretaker took our calls while we were away earlier this week. Please come in and let's get acquainted." She led us through a spacious entryway into a very large living room furnished with what came across immediately as elegant comfort and good taste. A huge Steinway concert grand piano graced one end of the room, with a variety of obviously very expensive bric-a-brac pieces and mini-sculptures scattered across both side and coffee tables. Floor-to-ceiling bookcases flanking a huge fieldstone fireplace and mantel, covered the opposite end of the room. Current copies of the Smithsonian and Atlantic magazines were strewn across two coffee tables.

We were ushered in to a love seat directly across from Blanche, who immediately plopped herself down with toes curled up under her legs like a kitten, arms around a huge pillow. There was a large bowl of freshly popped popcorn and other bowls of a variety of nuts, chocolate kisses and other tasties spread across both coffee tables amongst the magazines. Blanche reached for a bowl of miniature cookies and handed it across to us with a self-conscious giggle.

"Here, these are great," she said, "my mother made them just yesterday when she came by to see how our help's quarters are coming along." She turned around and looked out of one of the large French windows at the rear of the room. "Oh, there's where you might live once we get it all finished up," she said. "Would you like to have a look at what we're doing out here?"

We nodded an assent and followed her with handfuls of nuts and Hershey's kisses out through a gorgeously appointed kitchen to the rear deck which overlooked what she described would be her help's new quarters. We went down the deck's outer stairs and walked over to the two new buildings in which she had said "we might be living." Both buildings were planned to be, in appearance, almost duplicates of the large house, but in miniature. Ed and my eyes met one another, and we both mouthed the same words, "Wow, what a great place to live and work."

Currently their construction was at the finished plumbing stage, with considerable work left to be done with drywall, trim finishing and painting. There were two bedrooms, one bath with a Jacuzzi bathtub, a small living room and pleasant outer deck which also overlooked part of Lake Berryessa. The adjacent new building would be used by the help as a laundry, workshop, toolshed, and also a place to groom what she described as her prize-winning pygmy goats which, she said, she raised first as a hobby and now as a business.

"Come on out to the goat pen," Mrs. Terracline motioned with a wave of her hand ,"and see these precious little creatures." As we rounded the end of the under-construction building, a potent smell permeated the area. Fifty-plus little goats had created quite a mountain aroma.

Yet, in spite of the fact I had on my best pants suit I couldn't resist asking,

"Oh, how adorable! May I hold one?" Mrs. Terracline smiled broadly as she answered, "Oh, I was hoping you liked animals," and she scooped up one of the baby goats and put it in my arms. I was smitten when those big eyes looked up at me.

Ed reached over and patted the silky soft fur and asked, "How many goats do you have here."

"Oh, I guess I've got about fifty now. I sell some and then we have new babies all the time. I'd say we average about forty to sixty through the year. Oh, I haven't even shown you the rest of the house yet. Let's go back in and talk some more." Jackie reluctantly put down the tiny goat as Mrs T abruptly turned back up the deck stairs and led us back into the kitchen and thence on a tour through the entire huge home.

It had five large bedrooms, each with its own bath, a large computer room-library, an extensive recreation room complex complete with three satellite-connected televisions, two pool tables, and an exercise room with three stationary bikes and adjoining sauna and hot tub. A large L-shaped pool was outside the master bedroom, itself a showplace of casual luxury. I noted that the four-car garage currently housed a Mercedes sedan, a Mazda sports convertible. and a restored antique mahogany-hulled Chris-Craft power boat on a trailer.

When we were through with our tour, we sat down again in our original places. Ed commented to Blanche that her Steinway piano brought back many memories of his mother who had been a concert pianist, and I added that Ed played as well.

"Well, you will have a great time here with us on the piano if we can work out an arrangement," Blanche said. "We're gone so much of the time, you know."

Then I immediately came to the point. "Mrs. Terracline," I asked, "just what would be our duties if we were to come here and work for you."

She giggled that silly little giggle again, shrugged her shoulders and said, "Oh, the usual job, I guess; probably a lot like what you've been doing now. I'll need to have the house cleaned on a regular basis, of course." Looking at me she said, "And you will do some cooking, though we're gone quite a lot. My husband is a financial planner with a large international company and he has to travel all over the world. I often take trips with him."

Then I asked, " How much are you paying your help for this kind of work, and and just how do you schedule their time off?"

"Oh, you get the usual five-day-a-week work schedule with two days off each week. I've been paying our last staff couple here $2400 a month plus in-house living expenses, and the usual benefits like health and dental insurance."

"That certainly sounds very fair, and what days of the week do you find convenient to have for the help's days off? " I asked.

"Blanche puckered her lips a moment, apparently thinking out a reply. "Well, she said, "You could have Thursdays off and Ed could maybe have Friday or Saturday."

We both looked at her with raised eyebrows. "You mean we would each have a different day off?" I asked incredulousy.

"Well, yes," Blanche replied. "There has to be someone here every day to milk the goats and feed them their oats—and that's twice a day."

"You mean that taking care of all those little goats would be part of our responsibilities?"

"Why, yes, I thought you liked animals," Mrs. T. replied with a little puzzled frown..

Liking them and milking them twice a day is not the same thing. Ed and I looked at each other in absolute astonishment, simultaneously shook our heads, arose, and thanked Blanche for the interesting interview.

I said, "Mrs. Terracline it is really important for Ed and me to have our days off together because we need to occasionally to go back to our own home, and we need one another's daily support. And while we both are fond of animals, we are not now in a position where we must tie ourselves down to caring for dozens of them. We're really not farmers.

"I'm sorry, but I'm afraid we wouldn't be the people you need here. Many thanks for your time and courtesy in showing us around." Blanche Terracline looked both astonished and disappointed as we made our way out to our car. We waved a friendly goodbye and headed back to D'Arcy country.

"Well, one down," I said as we pulled away from the goats and oats.

For weeks afterward we would have laughing fits as we imagined one another milking fifty nanny goats twice a day. Well, maybe only thirty or so. The rest would have been billies.

Ironically, the very next day we noticed a lengthy story in the financial pages of the Sunday San Francisco *Chronicle* that was headlined "Franklin Terracline, well-known Bay Area financier, was indicted today for embezzlement of employees retirement funds." We both shook our heads at the story, telling ourselves how lucky we had been not to have been made goats ourselves.

That same Sunday morning we made our way over to Megan Branbury's place for our next interview. Approaching the property took us through several acres of well-groomed shaded lawns and flower beds and into a long curved driveway that fronted a huge English Tudor-style three-story house. We parked in the driveway near the front door, walked to the doorbell, rang, and waited with nervous curiosity to see who would answer it. We weren't disappointed.

Megan Branbury, slender and trim, very blonde, fortyish, with her golden hair in a long braided pigtail, and wearing smart Navy slacks and a white heavy, cotton knitted sweater with the sleeves casually pushed up to her tanned elbows, opened the door with a ravishing smile and a big hello. "Well, come on in! You must be Jackie and Ed. We've been looking forward to meeting you after our long conversation on the phone." She moved into the foyer of the house and then into a very large tastefully furnished living room. We followed, taking in every detail of this unusual home. At that moment a very tall, quite handsome young man—we guessed he'd be in his late twenties— entered the room with a big welcoming smile and shook hands with us.

"This is Marlon Clancy," Megan said. He lives here with me, and if he's a good boy I might even marry him." She tossed her head and long braid with a loud but quite genuine laugh as she stared directly at Marlon, who returned her amazingly brash introduction with a broad grin.

He was a strikingly good looking young man with wavy chestnut hair, deep blue eyes and an obviously easy manner about him. We guessed he was well over six feet with broad shoulders and tapering waist, and probably weighed at least 200. He seemed to be a perfectly built natural athlete. When he smiled, even dazzlingly white teeth radiated through a deep tan. He stretched out casually on a couch across from the two of us, one arm draped around Megan. The two of us relaxed on two deeply cushioned reclining lounge chairs.

Marlon had in his lap a clipboard and legal pad. He thumbed through several pages of notes, and then opened the conversation with, "You two are the 24th couple we have interviewed over the past three weeks. We are beginning to think that good help is impossible to find. But, now, just meeting you two may make us change our minds."

I replied, "Well, we are different from most household help, with professional backgrounds and being older than most people in these positions. But the past two years have given us a pretty solid experience and training in this kind of work.

"We have found that the biggest problem most employers in this field have is finding people who are not only well trained but also completely trustworthy. I think you would certainly find us to be that. While we may not have the panache of a professional butler, gardener, cook, maid or chauffeur—and we have filled all of those positions— we feel that we make up for it in integrity and industry."

"Oh, that's no problem," Megan quickly replied. "We live very simply and don't require a lot of personal attention. Since we have other properties both in the southern and northern parts of the State, and also up in Oregon, our main concern is to have a couple we can trust live here and see that house and grounds are properly maintained, and our cats and dogs cared for. Your duties. Jackie, would not include cooking, but occasionally helping me in the kitchen when I have a non-catered party. Really, it's just keeping up our house and pets, and the surrounding grounds. And whenever you have a problem needing extra help, you would be authorized to get whatever you need, whether it's an extra person, or equipment. We would start you at $2800 a month, plus your household accommodations and food, medical and dental benefits, with raises coming after a six-months' probation period."

Ed and I looked at each other with raised eyebrows and nodded to each other, with a kind of look that said, "We've got a live one!".

Marlon meanwhile appeared to be checking through our resumes. By now he obviously had figured out that we were in our sixties and seventies. He looked at Megan and she back at him. They both smiled at each other as he said, "Looks to me as if we may have found our help." Then, looking at us, he added, " What do you say we have a look around the place, and also see where you might be staying if you join us here."

The tour of the big three-story house was an experience vastly different from the overpowering impact of D'Arcy and George's place. But it still was magnificent. There were fourteen rooms. Each of four second-floor bedrooms had its own spacious bath.

There were two more smaller bedrooms with one bath on the third floor adjoining a huge attic storage area.

On the ground floor was a large cheery sunlit country kitchen-great room with new Jenn-Air range and other modern accouterments that occupied almost an entire end of the house. Throughout the home, beamed ceilings and plaster walls displaying pictures of English hunting scenes, early golf prints and other memorabilia of British country life gave the place almost the feeling of a well-worn but comfortable English old-country inn. Like most of the other large homes of the wealthy we had observed, this one also had a large grand piano in one corner of the living room.

An adjacent sports den was filled with glass-encased tennis and golf trophies apparently won by either Megan or Marlon, with littered desks for each of them on opposite sides of the room. There also was a pine-paneled, leather-trimmed bar with a huge television set at one end and a log-burning fireplace already aglow with a cheery welcome at the opposite end of the room. Bookcases filled another wall .

The two of them then led us out at the rear of the house and across nearly an acre of pine and oak-studded lawn, over a small wooden bridge spanning a winding small all-season brook that babbled quietly through the grounds in a fieldstone-lined channel, and finally to a white, green-shuttered cottage surrounded with rose bushes, stands of red-berried pyracantha and climbing wisteria. It was nearly entirely screened from the main house with trees and shrubs—-almost a Hansel and Gretel kind of feeling.

"This will be your place if you join us," Megan said, as we all walked through the glass-paned front door. "This is really a small apartment," she said, walking on through the place. "We use the other area for storage. Your quarters would be on this side of the house."

We walked through a small but nicely furnished kitchen and dining area, with range, fridge, and microwave installed with lots of adjacent cabinets filled with dishes and pots and pans. A chintz-draped window over the stainless steel sink and counters looked out over the sunlit surrounding gardens and a small orchard adjoining the cottage. The unexpectedly spacious living room was in a step-down section with a large projection-type TV at one end, flanked with bookcases. A huge antique pine armoire was at the other end of the room, with a couch, lounge chairs and drapes all beautifully coordinated with Pierre Deux fabrics and wallpaper. Small-paned colonial style windows behind the long couch offered a leaf-filtered view back across the property to the big house and adjacent pool. I noted also that there was enough room next to the armoir for a computer desk and accompanying accessories, something I knew Ed would find helpful with his writing. Floor and table lamps also were nicely coordinated with the rest of the cottage decor. The one small bedroom was similarly furnished. The entire layout simply radiated easygoing comfort. In fact, we later discovered that this cottage had once been featured in a San Francisco Sunday paper interior decorating supplement.

We liked the whole place, and were also taken with both Megan and Marlon. In fact, I think it was the cottage and the no-cooking idea which clinched our decision to take the job. I looked at Ed, and he at me again, we nodded, and that was it.

We all walked back to the main house as the sun was lowering in the western sky, its rosy light spackling the grass and little bridge with dancing spots of warm color. Fall was already beginning to make itself felt in the air. Somehow we felt that this could be our last job before we could finally go home and settle in to real retirement again.

Back in the house we shook hands and, amazingly, Megan threw her arms around both of us, saying, "Oh, we know we've got the right couple. We hope you feel the same way." Marlon followed her with another crushing hug and chuckle, saying "You guys will do fine. I know you will. Will you join us?" Being hugged by complete strangers who would be our employers really got to us both. It was amazing after our earlier dismal experiences.

Ed and I looked at each other, our decision clearly already made without even a conference. Ed said, "You bet; you've got yourself some help. When would you like us to start?"

Megan said, "As soon as you can get here. I realize you will have to give D'Arcy notice. So suppose we say that you begin with us here on October first? Do you think that would work out for you?"

I pulled my small calendar out of my purse, perused it a moment, and said, "Right now that looks pretty good. We first will want to go home for several days to check on how things have been going down there. Then we'll be back and begin with you folks. We'll stay in close touch in the meantime."

Floating on Air

Ed reports . . .

We drove back to D'Arcyville almost floating on air. No more stuffy fluff with D'Arcy or George. No more agonies with Greg or having to put up with nighttime clandestine poolside orgies. We were free!

Or were we, really?

The next day, a Monday, we gave D'Arcy notice that we were leaving . She never batted an eye or made one comment except to say, "All right, I'll have your final check for you on September 30."

A real cold fish, I thought, as she left the room and got on the phone again to her newspaper society editor buddy and several of her "breakfast club." No wonder young Greg was turning into a potential sociopath.

We drove the 220-mile one-way trip home that following week-end and found our house in good shape thanks to the care and concern of our neighbors. Hank Macintyre, the chap who had originally dubbed us "gutsy geezers," gave us both hugs and asked us if we were finally coming home for good. "No, Hank, " I replied. "Not yet. But we're gaining on it; we figure we'll be away probably for at least one more year. We think we now have an ideal place to work and good people to work for. Rest assured, we'll be in regular touch with you guys down here while we're gone, and we'll be home occasionally. We sure appreciate all you've done to keep our place in such great shape."

We still missed seeing old Smiley, our beloved cat, who always had greeted us each time we drove into our driveway. And going through our house, abandoned for such long periods, put us both in a temporary depressed funk. Our other big home still remained unsold, though our real estate agent felt that with another reduction in price and improving loan interest rates we should have it sold before too much longer. There had been some action on it while we had been gone. Only our earned income had kept it from being already foreclosed. In reality, we had been working away from home all this time so that we could pay for two homes, neither of which we could yet live in. It was truly a bitter dilemma.

But once we had checked out everything, and feeling fairly certain that we'd really be back home for good within a year, we headed back up to D'Arcyville for our last chores there before moving over to the Branburys.

We moved in the middle of the last week in September when neither D'Arcy nor George were around. She had left our last paycheck in an envelope on a kitchen table, with just the name "Hibler" scrawled on the envelope. No note, no word about Greg, no comments, no thanks. Nothing.

We called over to Frank Bartoloman to say goodbye and he rushed over to the house for a goodbye. We had really become fond of him during our stay with the Langstons, and hated to leave him. But we would only be less than a half hour's drive from his place anyway.

"I'll miss you guys, but I think you're smart in getting out of here. It will never get any better." He gave us both a big grin and hug, said he'd come on over to the Branburys some day and have a reunion.

Then we drove out of the Langston's life forever.

Branburyville—Another New Beginning

Ed reports...

Our move-in arrival at Megan and Marlon's place was un-eventful. Both of them greeted us warmly and Marlon even helped us unload our two vehicles. In less than a week we began to feel that we were nearly settled into both new routines and our new "home."

During this time we had chatted with next-door neighbors when we had gone to the front of the property to check mail, and had learned a great deal more about both Megan and Marlon. She had been divorced from an older nationally-known millionaire mover and shaker in the New York investment business before meeting Marlon. She also had inherited considerable wealth from her parents, now both dead, but currently worked as a real estate agent, specializing in million-dollar residential properties. She learned to find overripe but solid properties which were run down and needed upgrading. She would then make absurdly low bids for them, usually acquiring them easily, spending a few hundred thousand dollars to renovate them, then selling them for double or often triple her investment. A shrewd and canny lady.

We also soon learned that Megan had many friends of both sexes, and that she never was one to put on airs. The contrast between Megan and D'Arcy Langston was asbolute. As we spent more and more time with her and Marlon we began to appreciate even more her easy-going and friendly approach to dealing with people. We also discovered that she was exceedingly generous to friends and associates, and that included us, her new caretakers. She was always in demand as a speaker and we soon became accustomed to catching her occasionally on evening TV news with some of her many philanthropic works and charities, both local and statewide, especially those involving abused or neglected women.

We found that Megan had one child, a son now in military school out of state, who had lived with his father since her divorce.

We also learned that she was an excellent horsewoman, a crack rifle shot, loved cats, dogs and expensive cars, and that she casually wore a priceless collection of jewelry as if it were five-and-dime stuff. We often found diamond bracelets, rings and pearl necklaces all over the house—plus hundreds of dollars of loose currency stuffed in drawers or tucked into niches in the kitchen or under the TV in the den.

"I like to have it handy," she once explained.

Despite a superficial impression of her as being somewhat vain and self-involved, we discovered that she also was a widely admired interior decorator and home planner, with an intimate knowledge of both the mechanics of home construction and the art of exquisite decor.

Marlon was a quite different study. We discovered that while friendly and easy going, he liked to dominate those around him—except Megan who never permitted anyone to dominate her. He was fond of porno reading materials —he left it lying around the house—and, like Megan, was crazy about racing cars, and owned two collector's-item Bugatti and Ferrari models tucked away in the adjoining barn. Nothing like George Langston's collection, but both probably worth several hundred thousand dollars. He also came from wealthy parents, though not in the mega-rich strata of Megan's family.

We saw no evidence that Marlon had ever finished college or had held any kind of a steady job. Rumor had it that he either was asked to leave his college because of an affair with a female professor, or he flunked out, or both. After we had known them both for a while, it seemed that his days were mostly spent either on the golf course, tennis courts, reading the Wall Street Journal, or flirting with the many women at his golf club who apparently found his striking masculine charms irresistible.

In this regard, tolerant and liberal Megan, apparently realized that because he was at least ten years her junior, he needed more erotic dalliances than she did. Hence she for a while tended to make excuses for him. We guessed that he was properly dutiful in her bedroom, despite other temporary attractions. We wondered if they ever would actually marry, or how long she would put up with such playing around. However, they both seemed to truly enjoy one another's company and were forever going off on long week-ends either to visit their other homes, or some special watering hole like Lake Tahoe or a quick flight to Hawaii.

As we learned to keep up the large house and take care of both our indoor and outdoor duties, we found that both of them were in their personal habits a lot like unregenerate teenagers. They left clothes all over the house or in the yard by the large pool; money, as noted, was casually dribbled throughout the place. I'd find garden tools left on the lawn in the sprinklers, or a designer T-shirt draped over a shovel stuck in garden dirt. Jackie one morning found a woman's imported watch, heavy with diamonds, lying open in a bureau drawer with paper clips, single socks, an occasional tampax, and other female household detritus. It could just as well have been a Cracker Jack prize.

In fact this was one thing that continually struck both Jackie and me as we worked with all these differing people of great wealth. Though they all were quite different in their personalities and tastes, without exception none of them that we had known ever seemed to have any idea of what most middle-class people take for granted— the idea that possessions of whatever type should have care and maintenance. Clothes should be kept clean; neatness to us is a virtue. And maintaining things—cars, household equipment, clothes, etc. and fixing them when they break down, is part of a satisfying life. But these rich folk never seemed to worry about maintaining or fixing anything. If it broke down or looked a little worn, they threw it out and got a new one; cars, clothes, personal possessions—sometimes even people. Money was no object or ever a problem with anything.

One day in rearranging some cabinets in Megan's office part of the big den, I ran across a portfolio lying open on her desk. It was at least an inch thick, and contained listings of investments that her City broker had mailed to her. These were lists, page after page—up to nearly 150 pages—of single-spaced names of stocks, bonds and other securities. Stocks were often purchased in blocks of thousands of shares. The list included virtually every known blue chip securities investment listed in any Wall Street offering.

The value of such investments must have run into the many millions of dollars, though I never attempted to try to figure it all out. It was really none of our business. One thing was immediately clear: no matter how much money she spent, her investments kept adding even more and more income for her. Meaning that her biggest problems were clearly connected to somehow avoiding taxes on the steadily increasing volume of money coming in from such a massive investment portfolio. This was where her money management guru came in.

In fact Megan apparently never personally paid a household bill. We would pick up the mail every morning and distribute it to her and Marlon on their respective desks. Common household bills like electricity and gas would accumulate on her desk sometimes for months before she would finally put them all in a large manila envelope and mail them down to her money management guru in San Francisco who took care of writing checks and paying bills for her. I don't believe that she ever wrote a check—except for cash—for anything. Her manager did it all. In fact I doubt if she ever had any idea of what her monthly bills amounted to, anyway. She simply never saw them. Who cared, anyway? The whole lifestyle was eye-glazing to us both.

One morning Megan called us into her little den-office and told us that she owned a large "spec" home, now unoccupied, situated on the top of a mountain ridge overlooking the ocean, about twenty miles west of town. She wanted to take us both up to it because, though she had it for sale, it would need some maintenance as a show house.

Both Jackie and I piled into her red Rolls Corniche convertible with her for the half-hour drive to the place. Driving the Rolls like a hot-rod with the top down , Megan, long blonde hair flying, gave us a windy but sparkling drive up through coastal mountains to what proved to be a spectacular home astride a narrow ridge with a direct view of the Pacific Ocean.

The place was a fairly new 5000-square-foot, one-story French provincial country home with a Mansard rust-colored tiled roof, part of which was electrically movable for opening on sunny days.

As we walked up the front pathway to the door, Megan told us that she had purchased the place as an investment about a year earlier, and expected eventually to clear "four-hundred thousand" on it.

After first neutralizing an elaborate burglar alarm system, we entered the front through a large stained-glassed door, and found ourselves in a spacious entry hall with a wine-colored slate floor. The house was completely furnished with many period antiques, a small baby grand piano, and a huge French country dining room table with matching hand-carved chairs and a large pine hutch. A massive stone fireplace in the split-level living room faced an elaborate 18th century breakfront containing priceless collectors-item silver pieces and china.

Three large bedrooms with adjoining baths and Jacuzzi tubs were classic French provincial in decor. Hunting scenes and prints decorated the walls, with drapes matching the bucolic surroundings. The large country kitchen was furnished and equipped with the latest in appliances, with a special indoor barbecue built in to one wall.

Outside the master bedroom was a flagstone wisteria-covered terrace leading down to a very large, irregular-shaped black pool with diving board and a children's slide. The view from the pool to the west and south was spectacular. It was a very clear day on this visit, and we could barely make out the outlines of downtown San Francisco to the south, some 50+ miles away, with the Farrallon Islands barely visible to the southwest. The forest-covered coastline fell away to the north. A truly spectacular place with virtually no other home visibly nearby.

Back in the house Megan told us that she would like us to

come up here at least once a week to check out the place, keep the dust off furniture, and I was to keep weeds out of the several flower gardens now brilliant with vari-colored petunias and marigolds. "And if you feel like it, go ahead and hop into the pool if it's warm enough," she offered.

One thing we had noticed as we went through the house was that bedroom closets were filled with both men and women's clothes, some of them still with sales tags on them. Megan explained: "We lived here briefly when we first bought the property last year, and we keep nearly complete wardrobes for both of us in each of our properties." With other homes in flossy La Jolla near San Diego, a place near Mt. Hood in Oregon, another ski chalet in Aspen, Colorado, and a home in Hawaii, this meant that they must have had four to five thousand dollars of clothes in each of these places. Again, mind-boggling.

In fact, as we were leaving the house to go back to our valley place, I noted that the separate three-car garage had a pile of men's clothes thrown in a heap on the floor. Out of curiosity I picked up a rumpled camel's hair sports jacket with leather buttons from the heap, and tried it on. It fit perfectly—a size 42 long, and looked virtually new. The label inside read "Nieman-Marcus." Probably a $400 coat, I guessed.

Megan, watching me with barely concealed amusement, said, "Oh, those clothes belonged to my ex-husband. If you can use anything there, be my guest. I was planning to throw the whole bunch of them out anyway. When you come up here again, I'd appreciate it if you 'd get rid of the stuff. I don't need more reminder's of a dismal marriage."

I looked at Jackie with raised eyebrows, saying "Many thanks. It looks as if your ex-husband and I wore about the same size clothes." I later went through the pile and found several pairs of slacks, two other sports coats, several golf caps from places like Palm Springs and Banff Hot Springs and Napa's Silverado Country Club, everything virtually brand new. There were a dozen white dress shirts still in boxes, half a dozen sports shirts—all exactly my size, and ten pairs of shoes, but none of them could I wear. The profligacy —yet generosity—of these folks continued to amaze us both.

The addition of the mountain house of course added to our work loads, but because we had been promised extra help if we needed it, it really never became a burden. In fact we were beginning to feel almost like members of Megan's family.

Quite often at dinner time, when these autumn days were short, we would hear a knock at our cottage door and there would be Marlon with an arm load of steaks or pork chops, saying they had cooked up more than they could eat and wanted us to share what they had left over. Or whenever they had a barbecue with friends invited over around the pool, we were almost always included as guests, not servants. In fact our lives with Megan and Marlon were such a contrast with D'Arcy and George, or even Sin-Bed and Ada, it was hardly believable. And Lulu and Burnsy— well, they were on another planet.

Canine Surprise

Jackie reports . . .

I guess our first crisis with these two unusual people came scarcely a week after we had arrived. Marlon, who had somewhat impatiently run us through the intricacies of their elaborate home alarm system, told us that he and Megan were going to be gone for several days, but that he wanted us first to get acquainted with their new Jack Russell terrier pup which he had just bought as a special surprise birthday present for Megan.

He went out to his Bronco and reached into the back of the tailgate only to have the little black and white dog, yapping happily, leap out from under him and onto the driveway. In a split second the pup had raced around the house across the huge yard, and out into the busy street fronting the house. Brakes screeched, tires screamed, horns blew and the pup, happier than ever at all the excitement, raced back into the yard and up to a dish of table scraps Marlon had placed on the driveway by the Bronco.

Marlon grabbed him just as Megan came out the back door wondering what all the excitement was about. Marlon handed the squirming pup to her as she shrieked with joy, first holding him up over her head and then close to her bosom. "Oh, you little doll, you," she gushed. Marlon watched with a big grin, saying "Happy birthday, Meg. Hope you like the little tyke."

"Oh, I do. He's the cutest thing I've ever seen." She threw one free arm around Marlon, planted a big kiss on him, and the two of them went into the house with the wriggling puppy.

Now what, we wondered. We knew they already had two other hunting dogs they kept out of town in a kennel, and there were two cats around the house. But here was another responsibility. At least it wasn't another Greg, I thought. And it was cute, though intensely active and yappy.

The two of them left shortly thereafter en route to their Oregon place, waving a cheery goodbye from Marlon's Bronco. They apparently preferred driving the rugged Ford rather than the opulent and fussy Rolls on trips like these.

Less than two hours after they had left, with the new unhousebroken pup supposedly locked into a small fenced-in area outside the den door, we found him missing. Gone, vanished. Less than three months old, the pup hadn't even been named yet, with no collar or ID, he was Megan's birthday present, and we were responsible for keeping him safe and out of trouble.

It was now dark, and we found ourselves with flashlights roaming the neighborhood streets whistling and calling with no name, "Here, pup, here puppy," to no avail.

I looked at Ed saying, "Well, we haven't even gotten our feet wet here yet, and now we've lost Megan's birthday present. Looks as if we can kiss this job goodbye."

We called the police, three local vets offices, and the animal shelter with a description of the pup. But without even a collar on, it looked as if he'd never survive the maze of heavy traffic on nearby streets.

It was after midnight and we had spent three hours of fruitless calling and roaming the neighborhood. We finally fell into our cottage bed, but got little sleep that night.

The next morning we went over to the big house, punched in the alarm code and immediately set off an alarm that brought the police screeching in within five minutes. Shades of Lulu's place! We'd somehow goofed up Marlon's hurried instructions.

The police left and we simply shut off the alarm system so it wouldn't go off again during their absence, and continued to roam around the neighborhood calling "Here, puppy," with no reponse. Ed finally went out to work on the flower beds and to do some fruit tree pruning while I gloomily dragged myself up the long stairs to Megan and Marlon's spacious bedroom with its huge custom-made oversized four-poster bed, and began my cleaning routine. Of course they hadn't made the bed before they left, so I set about pulling it together.

The bed was at least two feet higher than a standard bed and I had to get a small three-step stool to reach it all. As I tugged the big down comforter back over the top of the bed I thought I heard a strange sound coming from under it. I got off the stool and bent down to peer under the bed but could see nothing unusual. As I raised up I found myself face to face with a happy, wiggling Jack Russell puppy, blankets draped over his head. He had been in this huge bed all this time while we had been wailing across the neighborhood looking for him. He had also doo-dooed all over the inner sheets, leaving both a mess and a potent odor to waft through the house, plus having chewed the satin sheets into shreds in several places.

But we were so glad to see him we hugged him, smelly or not, and took him immediately down to his contrived outside kennel for a hose bath and where we could watch him every moment. Ed went immediately to the local hardware store to get him a collar, leash and some puppy food—which Marlon had neglected to get, while I spent several hours trying to clean up the bed mess. One crisis down, others coming up.

Double Trouble

Ed reports . . .

As if one pup weren't enough trouble, a week after Megan and Marlon got back from their Oregon trip, he showed up one evening with another puppy, this one a gangling four-month-old black-spotted Dalmatian which he had named Dolly. Dolly and Russ, the obvious name for the Jack Russell..

This time Marlon drove into the yard in his Bronco with the new dog already collared and leashed—and for good reason. He had bought the dog from a friend who already had several others, telling Marlon that he was getting to be too much to handle—nervous, restless, constantly in motion. He thought Marlon's place with all the land around it would be a good place for Dolly.

Marlon got the dog out of the Bronco and took the leash off of her. For a moment she stood there not realizing she was now free. But in seconds she exploded in a wild run across the huge yard, around the pool half a dozen times, into the open garage, and back out for another incessant spell of running. Marlon kept yelling. "Here, Dolly, here Dolly," and slapping his legs, but the wild pooch paid absolutely no attention. Finally, after fifteen or twenty minutes of continual action, she trotted up to us, tongue lolling out of one side of her mouth, and sat down, panting heavily.

Jackie, who had just come out to witness all the wild canine activity, said to Marlon, "You have to be kidding—not another puppy! How come?"

Marlon, with Dolly now firmly leashed, said, "Well, Megan and I love dogs, and she has always wanted a Dalmatian. They used to be coach dogs, you know, and ran beind coaches or between the rear wheels of carriages. Nowadays they're often mascots for firemen and you sometimes see them riding fire engines with their masters en route to a fire."

Jackie nodded with not much enthusiasm saying, " It is really difficult now trying to keep the house in order even though I run the vaccuum every day over the carpets and furniture, and with Russ chewing up everything and leaving his hair and puddles all over the house, now here's another untrained pup. . . . I don't think this is. . ." Marlon interrupted her with a wave of his hand, Saying, "Well, that's what you guys are here for, to take care of that kind of thing," and walked off into the garage.

Jackie just glared after him in frustration.

We discovered that the dogs added at least 50% to the labor of trying to keep the huge place clean, because both pups were given the total freedom of the whole house—plus the two cats who slept anywhere from the top of the kitchen cabinets to inside the grand piano.

Then, one morning as I was leaving the cottage to go down the street to a nearby nursery for some plants, Dolly came roaring around a corner of the house behind me, knocking me off balance. Unbelievably, she grabbed my wallet out of the back pocket of my jeans, and took off with it. By the time I had picked myself up, cussing the miserable mutt, she had disappeared completely. My wallet with credit cards, driver's license and some cash had totally disappeared.

Megan and Marlon were away for the day at a golf tournament somewhere and I spent most of the rest of the afternoon searching for both the irrational dog and my wallet. Finally, late in the afternoon, I came upon Dolly lying under a pile of lumber on the far side of the property, still happily chewing on my wallet. She didn't attempt to escape or interfere, but just wagged her tail agreeably when I whipped what was left of it out of her mouth. Credit cards with deep teeth marks were scattered across the yard. My license had disappeared, and what money had been in it was probably giving Dolly twenty bucks worth of indigestion. I hoped so.

Megan and Marlon appeared upset later when I told them what she had done, and they quickly replaced my lost money—perhaps a twenty-dollar bill or so. But I still had to apply for replacement gasoline and other credit cards, and to go through all the red tape to replace my driver's license. I was beginning to hate dogs.

Then, the following morning, I was seated outside our cottage in our little patio area having an early morning cup of tea, when Dolly trotted up to me, whined briefly, then put her head in my lap, tail wagging, as she stared directly into my astonished eyes. I loved dogs again.

But I think the climax of our dog experiences came several months later when Megan called us in to tell us of a great party they were going to throw for Dolly's first birthday. It would have a fireman's theme, guests would all wear firemen's hats, and Marlon had already paid some $700 to have a rented antique fire engine drive into the place, siren wailing, with him and Dolly topside, to get the party rolling.

She asked Jackie to help her briefly in the kitchen, and me to assist Marlon and two friends with barbecue duties for an estimated one hundred guests. The Banburys were widely known in the area, and their parties were legendary. We expected quite an experience, and weren't disappointed.

Even though we both had supposed party duties, Megan told us that we were also guests, and to circulate freely among the others and have ourselves a good time. She gave us our own plastic red fireman's hats and told us to expect our first arrivals about six in the evening.

This being late autumn, nearly Halloween time, it was almost dark as our first arrivals drove in. I helped get people parked and cocktailed while Jackie and Megan worked side by side in the kitchen on gorgeous platters of hors d'oevres. Adding to the festive board were huge platters of a variety of 5-pound size cheese wedges. We had Gogonzola, Brie, Neuchatel, Roquefort, Stilton, and half a dozen others whose names I either couldn't pronounce or spell.

There was a special table with more than five kinds of bread to go with all the cheeses and fruit. We had plates of fresh seedless grapes, four kinds of apples, new pears and a huge bowl of late season strawberries.

The party was soon rolling with tri-tip beef, trimmed pork roasts and beef filets sizzling on three barbecues, and a Hawaiian-style bamboo bar serving not only the usual cocktails and high-balls, but several cases of champagne and cold duck all set up alongside the big pool.

The trees surrounding the pool were festooned with colorful paper Japanese lanterns, and all ninety-plus guests wore their plastic red fireman's hats, waving them in the air as they all sang USC, UC, and Stanford football songs, plus a few saltier ditties dreamed up by Marlon. Megan had a small spinet piano hauled to poolside and I and a couple of other guests, between songs, played some cocktail piano while we waited for all that gorgeous meat to be served.

Suddenly the sounds of our music were rent with a screaming fire siren at the front of the house. The whole crowd surged around the end of the garage to witness a chugging 1918 fire engine, complete with big brass bell clanging and siren screeching away, just pulling up to the front door. Aboard, as drivers, were Marlon, who had sneaked out of the pool after his randy singing, with happy Dalmatian Dolly alongside, tongue lolling out of one side of her mouth, her special fireman's hat askew over one ear. With one final screech of the hand operated siren, the assembled guests, glasses in hand, toasted their approval and made their way back to the barbecue and bar.

Dolly, her hat now dangling under her neck, raced down off the engine ahead of the crowd and snatched a large filet right off the barbecue, running happily across the back lawn towards our cottage. No one bothered to chase her. The party rolled on .

Then Russ, the Jack Russell terrier, suddenly came yapping into the crowd and ran up to Marlon who was chatting as usual with half a dozen gorgeous women around him. The dog kept up his almost frantic barking, running towards our cottage briefly, then back to Marlon. He made such a continuous fuss, clearly wanting Marlon to follow him, that he and I and a couple of his lady friends followed the frantic little terrier across the yard and bridge to our cottage. He raced around a corner of the building and stood yapping steadily by a large pyracantha bush. There, hanging on a snag of the bush, was Dolly caught by both her collar and the elastic cord of her fireman's hat. She was clearly strangling and jerking wildly, trying to get free.

Marlon quickly pulled her off the bush and momentarily laid her on the ground where her eyes seemed to begin to glaze over.

"Got to get her to the vet—quick," Marlon yelled. He scooped up Dolly in his arms and raced around to the garage where the Bronco was parked outside. In he leaped, and I got in the back seat, holding Dolly in my lap trying to stroke her and talk to her. We roared off with screeching tires about three blocks from the house to the vet's office. Fortunately his place was always manned 24 hours a day with a custodian, and he let us in instantly. He called the doctor at home and he showed up in less than ten minutes.

Meanwhile Dolly was barely breathing, twitching and jerking violently. Doctor Mulligan arrived, gave her a quick once over, and immediately gave her a shot of some kind. Amazingly, we watched Dolly tremble a bit, lick her mouth, and suddenly lift her head with a subdued whimper.

"You had a real close one, little girl ," said Doc Mulligan, patting her gently. "How did she get this way?" he asked Marlon. He told her about Dolly's snatching up the filet and galloping off with it.

"She apparently caught her collar and fireman's hat as she raced around the corner of the house by that pyracantha snag. If her buddy, Russ, our Jack Russell, hadn't come hollering to us she'd have strangled."

After about half an hour of heavy breathing, Dolly got up to wobbly feet and we hauled her back to the house.

The rest of the party had really swung into high gear after the desserts of self-made hot fudge sundaes from two frozen yoghurt machines Megan had brought in for the party. Only three people fell or jumped, clothed, into the pool during the whole evening, and by two a. m. the party had melted away.

Dolly, apparently no worse for wear, jumped back up into the fire engine's driver's seat and fell asleep. She really belonged there.

The last guests to leave were our next door neighbors Nigel and Mitzi Grover. We had already met them a couple of times at our mail boxes and had found them a fascinating couple. Nigel was very British, at seventy-two, tall with sparse white hair sprouting through a deep weathered tan. He was a retired senior vice-president and West Coast manager for an English exporting company, and now an American citizen. Mitzi, forty-fiveish, was a tall, ravishing, bubbly green-eyed redhead who had been a former Las Vegas showgirl. She still looked and acted the part, especially when she was around other men. We chatted briefly before saying good night and heading back to the cottage to fall into bed after a very busy day.

Ed reports:

Party Time

The next morning our phone rang before we went over to the big house to begin the after-party cleanup. I picked up the portable phone and walked out into the adjoining patio in the orchard. It was Mitzi.

"'Morning, Ed," she drawled in her dusky Oklahoma accent. " How'd you survive the party?"

"Great, Mitzi. You're up early, so you two must not have slept in very late."

"Yeah, but Nigel's still in the sack. Gotta get him up and moving." Ah, there was that difference. Seventy-two and forty-five! Energy! At seventy-one myself I could have slept in that morning, too, but duty called.

Mitzi continued, "Say, you two seem to like parties, right?

"Well, yes," I replied, "as a matter of fact we had a very busy social life before we got ourselves into a financial fiasco that caused us to have to go to work these past few years. We have really missed having parties and going to them. What do you have in mind?" I had the feeling that Mitzi, the party girl, was again up to her old tricks of making plans which were fun for her but not for bumbling Nigel. She was a dynamo, in constant motion, while Nigel, bored in retirement, usually busied himelf by endlessly adding on to their already sprawling house.

"Well, Nigel and I are having a big Halloween costume wing-ding here next week and we'd like you to come as our guests . . . and, uh, maybe you could you play the piano for us a bit? "

"Sounds like fun, Mitzi," I replied. "Let me talk to Jackie about it and I'll get right back to you."

I called to Jackie in the cottage kitchen, "Hey, Mitzi wants us to go to a costume Halloween party at their place next week. Want to go?" She beckoned to me through the window. I went into the kitchen door, and she said, "Are you out of your mind? We can't go to a party of theirs. We're hired help—and what would happen if they invited Megan and Marlon? Besides are you sure we are invited as guests or to serve and clean up?."

" No, Mitzi made it clear that we would be guests, although she did asked me if I would play the piano a bit. Since they will be having music for dancing later, that certainly wouldn't be a burden."

"What will we do for costumes?" Jackie asked .

"Honey, you can go as a cat— remember years ago at a party at home?——with black tights, a black turtleneck, painted on whiskers, and it seems to me you stuffed an old black stocking with something for a tail and you looked great. And I can wear that loud striped terrycloth bathrobe the kids gave me for Christmas, add a turban, a false moustache, and go as an over-the-hill sheik."

My enthusiasm was beginning to get to Jackie apparently. "Well," she said half in jest, "sometimes in this job I can't remember who or where I am. There are many times when I would rather be one of these rotten spoiled cats than to be the one cleaning up after them. So—let's go for it."

As it turned out, our employers were off the whole next week at Lake Tahoe with friends anyway, so on the party day—Halloween—at about sundown we walked through the gate in the fence that separated our place from the Grovers, and sauntered up the long curving flagstone walk to their front door.

Mitzi answered their loud bong-bong doorbell wearing a black and white French maid's uniform with a very abbreviated skirt revealing long, black-netted tapering show-girl legs. She had topped the outfit with a tiny lace cap and a very filmy blouse cut way down to there. As a well-endowed lady, when she walked she undulated splendidly, especially when she bent over in front of attentive men while serving trays of hors d'oevres. Several men, so served, spilled their drinks, or seemed to lose their orientation in Mitzi's cleavage.

As we arrived there were already fifteen or twenty couples there, most of whom were already well into their cocktails. Loud big-band music blared from what seemed like a dozen speakers all over the big rambling house. Nigel appeared as a British colonel (which he had been in World War II) in full uniform, complete with swagger stick and monocle. He was a great story-teller, and was in full delivery when we walked in.

As we came through the front door, Mitzi grabbed me by one arm and gave me what I was sure was a not-so-surreptitious thigh rub, and introduced me—and Jackie—to the other guests as "retired doctors of psychology and sex therapists staying with the Branburys next door. "

Jackie and I looked at one another, stunned at her brashness, but went along with her story anyway.

When Mitzi said "sex therapists" the men began migrating over to talk with Jackie.

"Sex therapists, *really?*" asked one portly man. "Do you use that cat outfit in your practce?" He smirked and tossed down the rest of his drink. "Where did you have your practice?"

Jackie lied very smoothly, "Beverly Hills!"

"Oh, my. You must have had some interesting clients down there."

"Meow— but we never discuss our clients."

Another attractive tall, graying lady with a mischievous smile, sidled up to me, took one arm, and purred , "Oh, you can tell me everything, Doctor."

I smiled back at her, shook my head, and said, "Sorry, doctor-patient privilege, you know." She backed off, sipping her drink but with a tell-me-more glance over one shoulder. Three of the men later left their business cards with Jackie as they left the party. "I think I could use your help," one man hissed as he sidled out the door.

Mitzi had decorated the entire big rambling house with orange and black accents, with pumpkins of all sizes and colors, cutout black cats, and dishes of candy corn scattered through every room. Nigel and a friend were aproned and doing the barbecue while Mitzi spent much of her time genuflecting in front of the men with her trays of goodies.

Most of the costumed guests were members of Mitzi and Nigel's well-established social group. The men were mostly retired or near retirement from their executive jobs with a variety of Bay Area concerns, and their women were apparently typical upper middle class chatty wives engaged in a variety of social activities. A vastly different group than D'Arcy and George's party-goers.

After a couple hours of eating and drinking, Mitzi swept onto the floor of the adjacent room she had cleared for dancing, and, after putting a tape into the stereo, went into a classic imitation of actress Shirley Maclaine. Instantly, she *was* Shirley Maclaine, long legs, red hair, the whole look. As a professional dancer Mitzi never missed a step of some memorable numbers, including pieces from *Forty-Second Street, Pal Joey,* and *West Side Story.* She sang with an amazingly good husky voice, tapped several numbers, and brought the house down with a lengthy, powerful performance of Ravel's driving, hammering "Bolero."

The whole crowd roared, cheered and shouted "More, more, Mitzi!" Even Nigel was on his feet roaring approval and applauding. But Mitzi now was beginning to wear down and begged off for a rest and another drink.

As she sank onto a couch next to two women friends, she suddenly passed out, and Nigel and two other men helped carry her upstairs to bed.

It was now after one a. m., and people were beginning to offer their thanks and drift home. Mitzi's sudden collapse suddenly dampened the rest of the party and it soon broke up.

Both Jackie and I were concerned about Mitzi and went upstairs to see if we could be of help. But Nigel, amazingly alert and concerned, was at her bedside holding her hand.

"She just wore herself out," he said, looking over his shoulder at us as we peeked in the door. "She's done this before; she just can't seem to get it through her head that she's not twenty any more." He got up from beside the bed, saying, "She'll be okay by morning. And thank you both for coming over. We loved having you."

We said our goodbyes, and made our way back down the stairs and out the front door. "Wow, what an evening," I said to Jackie as we walked back to our cottage.

"Meow," she said.

Uneasiness Sets In—With Another Party

Jackie reports:

Our daily lives now seemed to sweep by with ever increasing speed. October had come and gone; now it was nearly Thanksgiving time, with Christmas close behind. Our daily routines had fallen into set patterns that were predictable from week to week. I kept the huge house as much in order as possible with two wild dogs and two cats regularly destroying its decor, while Ed worked outside with the vast yard to be mowed, orchard to be pruned, and flower gardens, with occasional maintenance of fences, sprinkling systems and touch-up painting. Megan and Marlon seemed to just drift in and out of our daily lives as they moved from one posh nest to another. Actually, we saw very little of them during this time.

On week-ends we could occasionally get up with our old motor home into the Sierras near Lake Tahoe for a change of pace, but through it all we both were beginning to get more and more homesick, especially as the Holidays loomed ever closer. Though we had made trips home for check-ups twice since joining Megan and Marlon, every visit brought home ever more poignantly the fact that we were still, in effect, in exile

I looked at my calendar one morning and began counting out the days left in the year. Only thirty eight. And I wondered how many more months we'd have to stay exiled, away from friends and my dear very ill mother, now age 89 and hospitalized in Fresno with the after-effects of major surgery for advanced cancer, some 280 miles from us. I had always promised her that I would be at her side when she needed me. Now I was trapped in a totally unexpected dilemma.

Ed and I made a special 600-mile round trip to the hospital to see her one week-end, but came away fearful that we might not see her again. I had been feeling overwhelming guilt at not being closer to her, but circumstances seemed to conspire in our lives to keep us apart when we needed one another the most.

We found her in very poor condition, and her doctors pointed out to us that at her advanced age, there was little they could do now for her but keep her as comfortable as possible. We made our way back to our jobs in a cloud of gloom.

Then, the week before Thanksgiving, we got a lift with another party bid from Mitzi and Nigel, this time with a very formal engraved invitation. It read, *"Mitzi and Nigel Grover request the pleasure of your company at a Harvest Dinner Dance at the old Rossini winery, 4809 Harvest Road, Rosemont, at 8:00 p. m., Saturday, November 27. Attire semi-formal. R. S. V. P. Regrets only."* Mitzi had added in her own scrawl, "Come on over, you two; we'll have a ball."

A dinner dance? I hadn't been dressed for a dance in so many years I didn't know where to begin to get myself organized. Megan and Marlon had also been invited to Mitzi's party, but, as usual, they were on their way out of town, this time flying some 700 miles down the coast to Newport Beach to a flossy party of their own.

I had tried not to make an issue of my mother's illness to Marlon and Megan, but Megan, being a very sensitive and intuitive lady, had sensed things were not the same after our last brief visit home. I had nervously told her about our invitation and she excitedly went to her closet and brought out several of her dozens of elegant gowns, insisting that I try them on. Though she was an inch or two taller than I, with longer legs, we were otherwise about the same proportionally.

Megan said, "Jackie, it's time for you and Ed to get out for a fun evening, and I'll help you find something to wear." She then laid out four gorgeous designer dresses and a red silk stunning cocktail suit, any of which would have cost at least $500 or much more at a City palace of haute couture. I had never seen so many beautiful evening dresses and furs outside of a store in my life.

Megan seemed almost as excited for me as if I had been her sister. I finally selected that dazzling red cocktail suit. It fitted me amazingly well, though I had to do some adjusting on the pants legs.

Thanksgiving came and went, with all of our kids still spread across the country. Megan and Marlon went to their Oregon place to be with friends while Ed and I, for the first time in months, actually went out for Thanksgiving dinner at a nearby restaurant famed for its haute cuisine. It certainly wasn't like our old family gatherings, but we both enjoyed the novelty, and toasted one another with a bit of bubbly as we wound up a splendid meal.

Mitzi and I had exchanged phone calls since we received her invitation, and she was almost volcanic in excitement over her coming winery party. It was really to be a surprise birthday bash for Nigel, she said, describing the old Rossini winery, located on a country road well away from the Sonoma area, in superb wine-producing acreage, as being "the greatest spot for a party in all of northern California." We could hardly wait to see it. Just two more days to go.

Marlon and Megan left for their own extended week-end party the morning of Mitzi's. Then, just before they drove out headed for the San Francisco airport, Megan knocked on our cottage door, gave me a hug and handed me an envelope before dashing out to Marlon in his Bronco. She turned and waved to me as she got into the car and drove out of sight.

I couldn't imagine what she would be giving to me, but tore open the envelope. Inside was a lovely "friendship" card which she had personally hand-written. It read, "To my two most helpful and loyal friends. Have a ball at your party . . . Love, Megan."

Clipped to the card were three one-hundred dollar bills.

Both Ed and I were stunned. Never had we experienced such generosity, especially from an employer.

We went to Mitzi's party that evening, with me wearing Megan's gorgeous outfit and Ed, with no tux, making do with one of Megan's ex-husband's perfect fitting Navy blue sports jackets and matching slacks.

The Rossini winery turned out to be just what Mitzi had described. It was a huge rambling, ivy-covered fieldstone building with several wings that extended, finger-like, in several directions. Well over 100 years old, the place reeked of old-country nostalgia and the scent of fine wine. One of the winery's wings had been converted into an enormous bar and dance floor, with a log fire roaring away in a huge fireplace at one end of the long room. Dozens of giant wine casks and barrels lined the walls on both sides, with a myriad of red-checked gingham table cloths brightening up the room. Every table boasted a straw-covered Italian wine bottle with a lighted candle, trays of specially made Italian hors d'oevres, and several full carafes of different kinds of wine

As other guests arrived we noted several who had been at Mitzi's Halloween bash, with one of the men coming over to me, saying, "How about a little sex therapy, baby?" I felt like walloping him where he wouldn't forget it, but figured he already had more than his share of brandy and hard cider; but I mentally damned Mitzi for ever mentioning that Ed and I had done sex co-therapy together in our "other life." Now we were both targets for every kind of tasteless and inappropriate suggestion.

But it was fun, anyway. Mitzi had arranged for a small combo to play for the gala event, and the evening progressed nicely with many toasts to Nigel. Repeated choruses of "Happy Birthday, Nigel" echoed through the cavernous building.

Part of the band's repertoire included a number of latin numbers, and one in particular had always been a favorite of mine, the legendary Mexican Hat Dance. When the band leader, a mustachioed, handsome swarthy type wearing a big Mexican sombrero, announced the number, Nigel, who had been busy acknowledging all his birthday greetings, quickly got up from his chair next to mine and said, "Jackie, this one's on me." And off to the floor we went. This particular dance number always works up to a rhythmic crescendo, ending with a crashing chorus of brass and percussion.

Just at this point, Nigel and I, now alone on the floor, became the focus of the whole gathering. He gave me an unexpected sudden fast spin, I stumbled, and my pants fell off to the floor. The band repeated that brassy chorus while everyone in the crowd roared, laughed and applauded while I frantically tried to pull my pants back on. Apparently the adjustments I had made on that waistline were too generous. But at least the long beaded tunic kept me from being too blatantly exposed.

After finally getting myself pulled together, feeling the wine and the warm happy enthusiasm of the crowd, Nigel wobbled me back to my chair while Ed, sitting across from me, was still doubled up with laughter. It took him five minutes before he could stop laughing. That was one I'd never live down. But our evening was anything but over.

We laughed again all the way back to the cottage. En route, with the warmth and joy of the party still with us, I had thought that this might be a nice time for a bit of a loving rendezvous. I put on the only really sexy nightgown I had brought with us, went into the bathroom for a shower, hanging the nightgown on the back of the bathroom door. I had lighted a large party-type candle on the bathroom sink, was seated dreamily on the john when I suddenly noticed an orange glow flickering at the other end of the bathroom, and on the door. Not believing my eyes, I saw my sexy nightie going up in flames as it hung on the door.

"Ed! Ed!" I screamed, "Fire!"

As he slammed opened the door I raised up off the toilet and in all the excitement inadvertenly peed into my slippers. With the open door now up against the wall, Ed couldn't see the fire but kept looking for it past me out the window.

"Fire, where?" he yelled.

"No, no! It's behind the door, Ed," I screamed. He looked around the door, grabbed the burning nightie and threw it into the wash basin where he doused it with water.

Apparently when I had lit the candle and shaken the match to extinguish it, it had flipped unnoticed through the air onto the nightgown hanging on the door.

So much for the loving rendezvous. We spent much of the remaining night washing slippers and cleaning up the scorched woodwork of the bathroom.

Mitzi and Nigel's party had been a walloping success, and it was about the last of any recreational time either of us were to have for a long time.

Christmas and Sadness

Three days after the party, we got a phone call from Christy, my oldest daughter, that Mother was dying and to come home immediately. She was now out of the hospital and home for her last days. Christy and her other two sisters had been taking turns sitting up every night with her. We made arrangements with Mitzi and Nigel to feed and water the dogs and cats—Megan and Marlon were still away— and got into the old Datsun and headed south to Fresno.

Mother survived less than two days after we arrived, and was barely conscious enough to realize that we were finally home with her. Four days later we attended her funeral . Because she had been so well known in her community, there were several hundred friends and family members present to offer their condolences and support. After the funeral and a brief time with our daughters and other family members, we drove from Fresno back to our home in the foothills of Mariposa for another house checkup.

Things seemed about the same there, but now, after nearly four years, we suddenly had an offer on our other troubled house. Exhausted by all the turmoil, the loss of my mother, and the long drive, we told our agent we'd check it all out after we got back to our work. After the nearly 300-mile drive, we crashed into bed, noting that Megan and Marlon still had not returned home.

Christmas was now nearly upon us. During our visits with our kids at Mother's funeral we had asked them if they could be with us over the holiday. Ed's daughter, Caroline, her husband Ed, and Christy, Kathleen, and Melissa, my three single daughters, all said they would try to come up for a visit. So we had something special to look forward to.

The M and M's, as we were now calling them, were planning a lavish Christmas buffet dinner party four days before the holiday, after which they were again taking off or a two-week stay over the whole holiday period, this time at their Vail, Colorado pad. Megan had paid a special holiday decorator to completely deco-

rate the entire yard and house from top to bottom before her dinner party. It took him and his crew three days to get the job done.
Megan told us "it only cost $4500."

The decorating job took in not only a ten-foot lavishly decorated Christmas tree for the high-ceilinged living room, two smaller
trees in the den and dining room, but also long swags of ivy and
holly with tiny lights entwined around the stairway balustrades
and railings. Two huge hand-made holly wreaths were on each half
of the double front door. And multicolored Christmas lights ringed
nearly every window in the house on all three floors. In the front
yard area there were several lighted topiary animals, each twin-
kling with dozens of tiny blinking lights. On another side of the
house, a complete, nearly life-sized group of figures including Santa
Claus, his sleigh and all reindeer, were cleverly installed so as to
appear to be flying towards the roof of the house when lighted
after dark.

Yet, after all this elaborate decoration, there was no one home
on Christmas Day but Ed and I, and our grown visiting kids to
enjoy it. Megan and Marlon had had their big dinner party with
all their new decorations, exchanged presents with those friends
attending, then got ready immediately to take off for Vail. Before
they left I asked Megan what she wanted us to do with all the
decorations after the Holidays.

"Oh, either throw them out or donate some of the stuff to the
Goodwill people," she said as they drove out the driveway

Throw them out? In our families we kept Christmas decorations like family treasures from year to year. Here we threw them
out. But we actually did donate most of the hundreds of lights,
tree and other decorations to Goodwill.

We managed to have a wonderful Christmas day and dinner,
with most of our family with us in this enormous, super-decorated
home. Ed's oldest daughter, Lee, and her brother, Cliff were living
in Florida and Oregon respectively and couldn't make the trip.
But despite the festive time with those who were able to come, I
still was oppressed with the memory of my mother's passing. Some-

how it didn't seem right without her. I could never remember a time when she had not been with us on the holidays. Now she was gone.

All of our kids had to return to work at their homes, and suddenly we were alone in this big over-decorated mansion. Even next-door-neighbors Mitzi and Nigel were away in England visiting his family. We handled the sudden socially dead period by simply throwing ourselves into a heavy work schedule of working around the place, grooming and de-ticking the two dogs and two cats, taking them to their respective training classes, and dreaming for the time, soon, we hoped, when we could finally return to our own home.

By now we had considered the offer our agent had submitted to us on our unsold home, and decided to accept it. Originally, four years earlier, we had thought it was sold for $150,000, only to lose the deal when the buyers had their horrendous car collision. Over the next nearly four years three subsequent buyers, each at a lower price, had all for one reason or another, been unable to complete their deals. Hence, this final offer, this time not on a lease-option contract, but on a straightforward cash-and-mortgage deal, was for $97,000. It was a loss of more than $50,000, but now, at last, we would be out from under that eternal dead-horse extra mortgage payment that had been sucking us dry for years. It was finally over.

Trouble in Banburyville

Ed reports . . .

Megan and Marlon returned two weeks after New Years Day, ski-tanned and filled with stories of their stay in Vail. They complimented us on how neat and cleaned up the house looked—it had taken us a week just to take down all the decorations—and within a few days we were back to our usual routines. Megan spoke at fund-raising luncheons, Marlon played golf, read the Wall StreetJournal, and occasionally disappeared for the day, apparently out scouting around for more real estate possibilities, visiting the race track—or whatever.

One morning Jackie was working in the kitchen with both Megan and Marlon away for the day, when she suddenly smelled smoke. Walking hurriedly into the dining room from the kitchen she could see wisps of it coming from the front hallway. As she ran towards it she could hardly believe her eyes. There, in the middle of the foyer, was a massive, round antique French table with an inlaid leather top. In its center was a huge glass bowl, partly filled with water and long sprigs of curleycue willow branches sticking out of it. Intense sunlight streaming through the high windows over the front door had incredibly focused in the glass bowl into a hot spot on the leather table top and set it smouldering, just like I used to do as a kid with my grandmother's reading glass.

When Megan heard about it she shrugged her shoulders saying, it was old anyway. "Take it out to the barn and I'll get rid of it some time at a garage sale or something," she said.

Early in February Megan, already an accomplished cook, announced that she was going to northern Italy to attend a two-week course in Italian haute cuisine hosted by an internationally known lady gourmand well-known in culinary literature. On hearing this both Jackie and I agreed one evening that it seemed to us that the two of them were becoming more and more restless with one another. They were indeed spending a lot less time together than when we first met them.

One evening as we were watching a bit of television, we heard shouting from out around the lighted pool. I pushed aside the curtains a bit and could see the M and Ms by the pool, arguing about something. She was shaking her fist in his face, while he kept backing up towards the pool. Finally in a yelling rage, she pushed him off the edge, fully clothed, into the pool, and ran quickly into the kitchen door on the far side of the pool, slamming the door so hard a piece of glass fell from one of its panes.

We could make out only a few of the bits of the raging conversation before Marlon got his dunking, but it appeared that she was bawling him out for what she considered his excessive attention to one of her girl friends, all of which he was vigorously denying. Subsequently, Megan confided to Jackie that she was "up to here" with his messing around with other women, and that she had banished him from the house for a while. Her banishment took the form of sending him over to our cottage to occupy the other half of the duplex that had not been used in months. Thus for a couple of weeks we had to watch Marlon walking sullenly past our windows towards the other side of our cottage. It was clear that Megan wasn't kidding, but we wondered how long such a stand-off would last. After all, they weren't married, and with their pronounced age difference, plus Marlon's obvious randy temperament, things could unravel very quickly.

It was here that Jackie and I suddenly found ourselves inadvertently back in our counseling roles, with Megan regularly coming over to our cottage—when Marlon was away—for some earnest therapy.

In the next several weeks we were to witness several other incidents between these two that made it clear to us that the relationship would probaby not last too much longer. Megan began to make phone calls to old boy friends, and Marlon was spending more and more time either at the gold club, or at a race track near Oakland where he apparently was losing large sums of money on the horses.

The Flavor of Lyme

Then one morning I awakened with a frightful headache—and I just never had headaches—which got progressively worse as the day wore on. I took ibuprofen and aspirin to no avail. Finally, by the third day of it, with my vision now impaired and severe pain now spreading into every joint, plus a 103+ degree fever, Jackie, Megan and I headed for the nearest Kaiser Hospital. Megan drove for us and waited for most of the day while I underwent all kinds of tests to try an find out what was causing the sudden horrendous pain all over my body, with severe dizziness now added to the syndrome. A CAT scan showed no brain abnormality. Blood tests showed nothing wrong, but I did have a high fever, rapid pulse, and erratic blood pressure, plus a mild odd rash on parts of my arms and chest.

After being unable to find out what the problem was, they sent me "home" with advice to "drink lots of water, take plenty of aspirin or ibuprofen, and get bed rest." Where had we heard all that before?

It was clear that I could no longer carry out my work schedule around the house in this condition, and Megan had to hire someone to take over for me. Of course this sudden illness upset Jackie who had to continue to carry out her heavy work schedule, plus having to groom and pick ticks off the dogs and take them to their obedience training classes. I just lay in bed and moaned.

After about a week of this agony without either any worsening or improvement, I said to Jackie, "We can't hack this much longer. Let's go home. At least I can die in my own bed."

"You're not going to die yet anywhere," she replied. "But I think we probably should think about winding up this four-year survival experiment. Let's talk some more about it, and then discuss it with Megan."

Ironically, Megan came over to the cottage the very next morning, walked into our tiny bedroom and sat on the edge of our bed. She looked a bit wan and harrassed herself, and I told her so.

"Yes, you're right, Ed. I am harassed and frustrated. I've been telling you about the problems Marlon and I have been having, and it isn't getting any better. Also, I've been concerned about you two. As you are well aware, I've come to depend upon you both for more than just household help duties. . ." And here her eyes welled up with a flood of tears. "But I've been doing a lot of thinking. You've been here with us now for nearly a year, and I have decided that I just am not going to need full-time help here much longer.

In fact I have already put this place up for sale. As you know I buy and sell real estate for a living." She smiled and wiped her eyes with a tissue.

I looked at Jackie as I said to Megan, "This is really an incredible coincidence. Jackie and I last night were saying that with this crazy undiagnosed illness, I clearly can't carry on here with you and Marlon, much as we'd like to. Now you come in and tell us virtually the same thing."

Megan suddenly bent over the bed and gave me a long firm hug. "You'll get over this bug soon. I know you will. Let me know what your plans will be for leaving us and I'll work with you on helping you get organized and packed."

She stood up, looked at Jackie with more tears in her eyes. She also gave her a loving hug, turned, and went outside wiping her eyes as she went.

Oddly, both Jackie and felt that a bond was being broken, one we had never anticipated when we first had come here. Megan Branbury, a socially responsible woman of immense wealth, prestige, and social grace, had virtually made us members of her own family. We would never forget her, her generosity, and total humanity.

Spoiled? Yes, undoubtedly. But she carried her "spoilage" with such panache she had made herself an incomparable human being. And Marlon? Well, he was just Marlon and probably would continue to seduce and exploit women. Perhaps someday he might even search for some real meaning in his life.

Winding Down

Within a week after our climactic talk with Megan, though still in considerable pain and muscular weakness, I got the old motor home and car loaded, with Megan and Mitzi and Nigel's help—Marlon was who knows where— and was almost ready to head for home. We had to pinch ourselves to be sure we weren't dreaming. But, after nearly four years, we were actually going home.

The morning we were leaving, Megan came over to the cottage which was now almost back to its original Pierre Deux decor with all our stuff removed, quietly walked through the place as we watched. With glances at me she said to Jackie,

"This little place will always remain something very special in my memory, not because of all the special things I put here, but because two very special people made it into a home—a place where honest love and care really meant something. I will forever be grateful to you for what you both have brought into my life—and Marlon's too. Even though he's not here today, he wanted me to tell you he will miss you, and thanks you for your help with him, too." She quietly gave us both long hugs, saying, "Please stay in touch. I will miss you both terribly."

As she turned to go out the door she pulled an envelope from her purse and handed it to Jackie, saying simply, "Thanks," then turned towards her house. We watched her dejectedly walk across the little bridge that had become so much of our daily life here, and disappear into the kitchen door. Jackie and I looked at one another, both of us in tears, as Dolly and Russ suddenly bounded across the bridge to our cottage door.

Just how did they know we were leaving? We would never find out. Both dogs whined and wriggled around us for several minutes, seeking the pats and hugs we were now so used to giving them. When they had trotted back to the big house, Jackie tore open the envelope Megan had left with us. In it was another handwritten note, saying simply, "Thank you both for making my life so much easier. I love you. Go home in good health." Again she had attached one hundred dollar bills, five of them.

The following day, though still running a slightly lower fever, in chronic pain in every joint, and dizzy when walking, I still felt I was able to drive the old motor home now loaded with our stuff, while Jackie followed me in the Datsun. We drove slowly out the front Branbury gate, wistfully watching the big Tudor style house gradually melt away in the mirror, and headed for Mariposa and home.

EPILOGUE

We had used up more than three critical years out of our lives after being told we were crazy to try to do what we had done. We had survived four hysterical months of retirement home management, a broken leg and months of healing for Jackie, six weeks with crazy Lulu and Burnsy, nearly a year with starchy Sin-Bed and lovely Ada, nearly another year with devious D'Arcy and tiddly George, and now another year with wildly improbable Megan and Marlon. Where would we go from here?

The first place I went after unloading everything at home with neighbors' help, was to the Kaiser medical center in Fresno for further checks. After three days of more tests and evaluations, they finally found what had made me so sick: Lyme's disease; I had picked it up almost certainly from one or both of Megan's tick infested dogs who were constantly out in the high grass and bushes surrounding the estate.

But now we were home, really home. Every morning we awakened and looked out at our majestic ponderosas and oaks, and were filled with gratitude at what we had been able to do for ouselves. I was now nearly 74, Jackie 64. We geezers had hung on, and even though we still were in a tight financial spot, it was vastly improved. We had paid off one mortgage, put money in the bank. Yes, we had beaten the odds.

We are now 84 and 74 as this joint writing task comes to an end. Jackie and I are currently jointly teaching Memoirs Writing to a large class of seniors one day a week, and Jackie also does substitute teaching at a nearby elementary school.

We frequently speak to senior groups about the values of writing one's life story, and these experiences which you have just read here are but a fulfilling fragment of our own.

Oh, the same neighbors who had labeled us *gutsy geezers* said recently, "You two really are gutsy geezers; now you should write a book about it".

We did.

THE END